FAINT TRAILS

An Introduction To The Fundamentals
Of Adult Adoptee/Birth Parent Reunification Searches

by Hal Aigner

Paradigm Press

"(I)t seems to us that the conclusion is irresistible that an adopted child, in a legal sense, is both the child of its adopting parent and its natural parent. We reach this result not only because the overwhelming weight of authority in the United States points in that direction, but to hold otherwise would be extremely unjust and unnatural."

— In re Estate of Tilliski
Appellate Court of Illinois
Fourth District—June 1944
323 Ill. App. 490

Designer: Diane F. Dudeck

ISBN 0-937572-00-4

ACKNOWLEDGEMENTS

While gratefully remembering the many people whose support here and there over the past several months has helped to sustain this project, I would like to offer special thanks to those whose assistance has been especially crucial to its completion: Dr. Henry Aigner, Sandy Abbot, Helen Dreyfus, and Kathy Geiger for their aid in making production possible; Michael Goodwin and Louise Lacey for readings and editorial comment, and George and Bernice Smith and Jane Wittrock for production assistance.

Paradigm Press
127 Greenbrae Broadwalk
Greenbrae, California
94904

For Pat W. and Marge S.

TABLE OF CONTENTS

Introduction 11

    "17-Year Search Ends
    When Father Found"

Section I   31

    Amended Birth Certificates 36
    Adoptive Parents 39
    Delivery Doctors 41
    Hospital Records 44
    Church Registries 46
    Newspaper Vital Statistics
        Announcements 48
    Sealed Records Files 49
    Newspaper Advertising 51

Section II   53

    Telephone Directories 54
    City Directories 56
    Vital Statistics Offices 58
    Probate Records 59
    Voter Registration Affidavits 60
    Drivers License Records 63

Section III   67

Social Security Administration 69
Knocking On Neighborhood Doors . 73
Search Self-Help Organizations 74
The Assessor's Office 77
Veterans Administration 80
Job Opportunities 83

Epilogue 87

"Go For It"

Appendix

Major Western States
    Public Libraries 92
Sample Interlibrary
    Loan Form 94
Sample Sealed Records
    Court Petition 95
Piecing The Past
    Together 96

INTRODUCTION

"17-Year Search Ends When Farmer Found"

Comes a time for many groups with a message worth hearing when the world begins to listen. For familial reunification searchers, that moment may have arrived. As a result of more than 30 years of their individual initiatives, their desire for widespread consideration of their feelings and viewpoint has become difficult to refuse. Their progress has been appreciably well documented. Here and there for decades, the popular press has repeatedly drawn generally favorable attention to the drama of familial search and reunification. If you're interested in the subject and you watch headlines, then for some while you've been eyeing material such as this: -

Adoptee Meets Mother After 29 Years

Love Sustains Woman in Search for Son

Sympathetic Judge Provides Missing Link for Adoptee

Adoptee, Birth Parent Find Moment of Truth

Reunion After 35 Years

Below the headlines, the copy is usually of a type: a warmhearted 500 to 1500 words touching upon some of the emotions, struggles and rewards entailed in a search. Review a sufficient number of these articles and a few very vivid impressions take form. For one, after reading dozens of news reports, it is apparent that the need to search knows no social boundaries. At any given moment, among people who by chance or circumstance have been separated from members of their families, the need can prompt any person from any walk of life into action. Searchers can be rich or poor, young or old, anonymous or famous. They can even be Hollywood movie stars.

Marilyn Monroe was just such a person. Born Norma Jean Baker on June 1, 1926, the screen legend is best remembered as the blonde heroine of a classic, true-life Hollywood drama. In her early twenties, she emerged from a youth characterized by unusually severe domestic troubles to begin her career in the movies. Before her death, she worked with some of the film industry's leading directors, including Billy Wilder and John Huston, and some of its finest actors, including Clark Gable and Sir Laurence Olivier. By 1957, this nude pin-up girl of the late Forties had achieved such prominence that she was received in a command audience by England's Queen Elizabeth II. Along the way, she captured the public fancy as no other actress had done since the dazzling Jean Harlow.

And yet, in terms of the actual inspiration that Monroe's life continues to offer to thousands of people, Hollywood may merely be the backdrop against which another entirely different drama, far more important and far less conspicuous in its dimensions, was played out. Surprisingly enough, this blonde whom gentlemen preferred was an early family reunification searcher, much after the fashion of so many adult adoptees today. And in that tale may lie the enduring meaning of her personal saga.

True, the actress was never adopted. Instead, her early years were characterized by time spent in an orphanage and a series of 12 foster homes. But in the practical terms of a reunificaton effort, the similarities she shared with hundreds of current searchers outweigh the differences that would separate her from their ranks. As is common to most of those en route, she was born out of wedlock. Like the others she longed for connection with a missing birth parent; in this instance, her father. With the majority of them, in early adulthood, she embarked on this quest.

It took Norman Mailer in his complex 1972 analytical biography *Marilyn* to finally key the facts of Monroe's childhood and adolescence to subsequent events in her life. Her youth left her, he concluded, with an absence of clear identity— which, by the way, is a concern frequently articulated by many contemporary adoptive searchers. "Great actors," he then wrote, "usually discover they have a talent by first searching in desperation for an identity." He added: "A child who is missing either parent is a study in the search for identity and quickly becomes a candidate for actor (since the most creative way to discover a new and possible identity is through the close fit of a role)."

But in addition, if Mailer is correct here, and there is no ready reason to disagree with him, then his thinking only has to be carried a few steps further for Monroe's reunification quest to be brought into perspective as the crucial drama of her tumultuous 36 years. By embarking on this search she was implicitly attempting to do something about the lack of identity that so forcibly influenced her professional successes. Consequently, the outcome of her search was certain to have an enormous effect on the future that remained to her.

In the process the actress provided for all who were to follow a means of exploring the nature and dynamics of this entire business of search and reunification. Monroe's familial reunion story unfolded in a society that was ill-prepared for, and often openly hostile to, such undertakings. Almost 30 years have passed since she ventured forth and the social situation has improved markedly. By measuring the relative ease with which similar searches currently proceed against the difficulties surrounding Monroe's nearly three decades ago, it is possible for those who are presently engaged in reunification efforts to draw encouragement from this pivotal segment of her full legacy.

In 1951, at age 25, Monroe set out to locate the man whom she believed to be her father. She soon discovered that he lived on a 10-acre farm near the small Southern California town of Hemet, some 90 miles from Palm Springs. From her Los Angeles residence, she drove with a friend one day almost the full distance to her father's home. But as the journey drew close to its end, she stopped by a roadside phone booth and called ahead to announce her imminent arrival.

The memories she later shared of that conversation are painful and embittering. According to biographer Fred Guiles, her purported father apparently didn't even come to the phone; he spoke to Monroe through his wife. He did not deny that she was his daughter; neither did he acknowledge paternity. Rather, he insisted that he did not want to see her. If Monroe had a complaint, the man's wife echoed, she should see his attorney.

Assuming that the farmer was her father and that the description of the telephone encounter, for all its damning overtones, is essentially correct, it may still be possible to construct a mitigating explanation for the father's blunt rejection of his actress daughter.

From the late 1940s and into the middle 1960s, American opinion was for the most part antagonistic toward unmarried parenthood. The public morality then popularly portrayed unwed mothers as victims of thoughtless seducers. During and immediately after out-of-wedlock pregnancies, enormous pressures were brought upon parents to release infants for adoption, which would supposedly reduce for the child the burden of having been born a bastard. Failing that course, attempts were made to have the child reared exclusively by one parent, usually the mother. During those years, it was somehow viewed as improper and irresponsible for unwed fathers to care for their children.

There was one major exception to this attitude. Men were expected to be financially responsible for their offspring, even when they were deprived of having any role whatsoever in their children's upbringing. In those days, paternity suits were a lively and estranging legal activity. The measures were frequently vindictive and punitive in their results. A father could be forced, say, to provide child support and simultaneously be refused any part of his son's or daughter's custody and companionship. Over a broad span of time, such a practice helped cultivate the notion that any interest an out-of-wedlock child had in his or her father was purely financial.

Finally, in 1951, the adult drama of reunification between birth parents and the offspring from whom they had become separated years before was an exceedingly rare occurrence. It was also vigorously opposed as unnecessary and unhealthy by virtually every authority figure that could be mustered onto a common roster. Social workers and adoption placement agency representatives inveighed against such reunions. Lawyers, doctors, priests and ministers repeated the censure. A reunification was then an affront to convention.

So it is possible to comprehend Monroe's father as a product of his times. He can be seen as conditioned to react rather than to respond to the phone call from this stranger with a claim on him. Perhaps he had long forgotten that mutual love was one of the rewards he might have received by risking a relationship with the daughter he never knew. He may have believed that she could be nothing more to him than a threat.

Yet, when the situation is examined under the disturbing light of the actress' final moments, such gentle understanding becomes difficult to sustain. On August 5, 1962, after a life of extraordinary turmoil, Monroe committed suicide. Her career, as a substitute for a strong personality rather than an outgrowth of it, was successful, in part, for the wrong reasons. Eventually, professional achievement and audience acclaim alone simply weren't enough to sustain her.

The manner of Monroe's death cannot be detached from her father's indifference. For if author Mailer's contention that the problems of a confused identity were central to the Monroe personality, then the foreclosure of one of her few viable opportunities to diminish the confusion must have had a profound and debilitating effect on every aspect of her life thereafter.

The screen star had longed for the paternal connection at least since her adolescence, when she fictitiously insisted to friends that her dad was secretly matinee idol Clark Gable.

When suddenly dispossessed of even a reunification fantasy ... well, here speculation becomes too easy and conclusiveness becomes too elusive. Maybe other methods existed by which Monroe could have found her way back to emotional health and stability. But at present, a plentitude of reasons exists for believing that a reunification with the Hemet farmer in itself might well have done the job.

How true and easy it is to suggest that had Monroe's search taken place 30 years later, her reunification effort would have stood far greater chances of fulfilling her minimum expectations. Under optimum conditions, in fact, the personal gains she would have derived from the experience would have been more than minimal. Long before the 1980s, her search would have benefited from the reformation of social-sexual values that she herself helped precipitate. The circumstances from which she proceeded would have become radically different in her favor.

Perhaps most significantly, she would have found widespread practical support for her endeavor. At present, tens of thousands of adults throughout the United States are involved in reunification efforts similar to hers. They come from all walks of life. Their task is primarily one of records research. Beyond a common need to establish or renew familial ties, they apparently don't really fit into any particular psychological or sociological pattern.

Adult adoptees constitute the largest and most assertive segment of this movement. The rough statistics available from the country's more than 100 search self-help organizations indicate that there are currently between 100,000 and 150,000 people in this category. They comprise only a small fraction of the total number of adoptees in the United States. Federal government statistics, which are also very rough, place that figure at about 5 million. But the ranks of adult adoptees en route to their birth parents and siblings are expanding rapidly.

The second largest group is composed of birth parents, primarily mothers. Some search organizatons estimate that

> "At a reunion, Opal told Rosilee she remembered her big sister coming into her bedroom at the orphanage one night to comfort her, after the children learned they were to be separated. She said, 'When you get to be a grownup lady, I'll get hold of you and we'll be together.'"
>
> —*Reunification of sisters as reported in the August 30, 1978 St. Joseph Missouri* News-Press

birth mothers account for as much as 30 percent of their membership. These organizations often contend that women who have relinquished their infants for adoption never lose the desire to see the children once again and discover the person they have grown to be. The contention may be right, although it would be difficult, if not impossible, to verify sociologically. Not very long ago, placement agencies and other bodies opposed to reunifications insisted that searches were improper because it was in every instance necessary to protect the privacy of birth mothers. Through their action, mothers in search are consigning that insistence to a well-deserved oblivion.

The remaining portion of the movement is made up of people who are not yet widely associated in either the popular or institutional mind with search and reunification. Children of divorced families who have lost contact with one parent are included here. So are siblings who have been separated from one another through the processes of either adoption or divorce. Occasionally even a birth grandparent makes an appearance looking for a relinquished grandchild.

For each of these thousands, a search is, above all else, a

vital, living drama. Thirty years ago, a personal theater of this sort was isolated, naive, unskilled. But that, too, has changed with the passage of the decades. Over the years, from the combined stagings of hundreds of individual stories, important lessons have been learned. In their practical wisdom, they are neither philosophically surprising nor intellectually novel. Nonetheless, the contributions of security and solace that they can bring to the often unpredictable demands of a reunification effort are impressive. In short, since 1951, a refreshing availability of perspective on the search phenomenon has developed.

As one especially valuable example of this perspective, it has been learned that searchers who proceed on their own initiative, proceed most ably. The more knowledgeable self-help organizations wholeheartedly endorse that finding. Inside and outside these groups, experience after experience has demonstrated that people in quest are almost always their own best detectives.

Certainly, there are occasions in which private investigators may prove helpful. A professional practicing in a geographically distant area, say, may be called upon to pore through pertinent civic records within his jurisdiction. For that matter, lawyers and doctors may at times also be of assistance, particularly in situations in which they took an active part in an adoption that was finalized entirely outside the auspices of a placement agency. Under that circumstance, their office files may still contain a record of the proceeding.

But formidable problems can be created by the hiring of professionals to handle the probes and paperwork entailed by a search. Their commitment to the effort is of a different, and perhaps detrimentally different, order than that of adult adoptees and birth parents. They frequently produce no better results than searchers can produce for themselves. They are usually expensive. And what must be taken most seriously is that their employment can deprive adult adoptees and birth parents of the opportunity to discover, at the source, some of the deeper emotional causes underlying search activity.

Personally conducted searches evoke responses across a

wide spectrum of feeling. The elation of uncovering another clue is savored. The frustration of reaching a momentary dead end rankles. By observing these reactions closely, by watching the thoughts that are provoked and the mental images raised, searchers increase their awareness of who they are and why they are drawn to what they are doing. And through awareness, they gain understanding and release. It's a time-honored formula. Many people with questions about why they are so deeply impelled by the need to search, discover the answers they seek en route. That can never happen through a surrogate.

Another lesson learned over the years about searches is that the initial tone of reunification is not always indicative of what will follow. According to hundreds of reports, all of which have merged together into something resembling folklore, positive first moments with sought-after relatives normally lead directly toward positive, continuing relationships. But an initial contact that is uneventful tends to reflect transient inhibitions. And negative reactions are commonly known to reverse themselves in a matter of a couple of days to several months.

It is worth remembering that to birth parents reconciled to permanent separation from relinquished children, first contact comes as an upset to decades of habits, decisions and ethical assumptions. For a brief period, they are likely not to know what they think. They may be slightly stunned. In 1979, a woman of my acquaintance located her birth father in Idaho. She phoned; they had a brief conversation that seemingly had no effect on him. Disappointed, she hung up. Within a half hour, her father returned her call. His opening question was, "What you're trying to tell me is that you're my daughter?" The two continued on from there. Similar tales now abound throughout the country.

So today, Marilyn Monroe would likely have been forewarned against investing all hope in the opening hello to her father. In addition, particularly if she had affiliated with a search self-help organization, she would likely have also been apprised of the reasons for restraint. Her father's harsh reply to her telephone call might not have been his final word. A genuine possibility remained that the next day, or the following week or month, his attitude would have changed.

Continuing in this vein, according to rough self-help organization statistics, 96 percent of all reunifications between adult adoptees and birth parents are regarded by both parties as of some real, if intangible, benefit to their lives. Other sources dispute that figure, but not by wide margins. Significantly, material released by the New York headquartered Child Welfare League of America, traditionally a vigorous opponent of these reunions, reduces the number only to 87 percent.

All partisans seem to agree that two percent of all search efforts end with some overriding measure of unhappiness. Generally, the prevailing problem consists of an adamant refusal by the sought-after individual to establish any form of communication at all. Also, to a much larger extent, a quest occasionally ends with the discovery of a person so severely stricken by a pathological disorder that further contact is inadvisable and dangerous. It would be a mistake to embark on this kind of adventure without acknowledging that a small chance of disillusionment awaits.

For the remaining two to 11 percent, thoughtful, skillful script work can be decisive. In 1980 Monroe, alive and considering her next moves, would stand reasonable chances of finding a better avenue of approach to her father. Perhaps a visit to his lawyer would have proven useful. The attorney might have been able to intercede favorably on her behalf. Perhaps she should have mailed her dad a letter. The correspondence could have supplied him with her address, or phone number, and an invitation to reply when he was ready.

Perhaps nothing would have worked. But the search movement's accumulated experience warns clearly against foreclosing options before they are tried. Adult adoptees and birth parents currently relate, time and time again, success stories enlivened by a recounting of how events turned on the basis of some minor combination of imagination and perserverance.

"Ed Goldfader, founder of Tracers Company of America, a professional missing persons bureau, . . . said that people are no longer afraid to 'make waves.'

"'The women's movement changed all that. The black movement changed it. The student movement changed it. People don't sit back anymore. I foresee a situation in the future when all adoptees will look for their natural parents. I can't imagine a situation any other way,' Goldfader said."

—From the April 16, 1978
Barre, Vermont Times-Argus

Reduced to their simplest expression, then, the guiding principles of well over 100,000 familial odysseys amount to patience and persistence. As promised, they are not startlingly original. They are effective. As fundamental elements of a general philosophy of common sense, they have value everywhere. But in 1951 and, for that matter until as late as 1970, only a few people had the faintest idea of how these principles operate under the concrete challenges posed by a reunification effort. Today they are understood and applied on a widespread basis. By their informed use, the going has been made substantially easier for searchers throughout the United States.

Since the 1950s, however, maturation from naivete to the beginnings of sophistication has been only one change among the several that have brought search and reunification to its present status as a national movement. Giving credit where it is due, much of the way was prepared by what is now ordinarily referred to as the sexual revolution and by the feminist revival of the past two decades. Even the 1960s Civil Rights movement played a role here, particularly to the extent that it encouraged people to stand up for and act upon their personal dignity. Interestingly enough, there is no ready evidence that the proponents of those ferments ever had adoptive issues in mind when they pursued their goals. But their net impact on those issues has nonetheless been formidable.

Among the influential changes that preceded the growth of searching from a few to thousands was the virtual disappearance of the so-called "stigma of illegitimacy." It is difficult to imagine anyone caring a whit any more about entering into this world as a bastard. Certainly, adult adoptees considering reunification are no longer inhibited by the possibility of discovering that they were born outside of a marriage.

In legal traditions based on British Common Law, which predominate throughout the United States, bastardy has historically survived as an economic status defined and enforced by statute. Its original function was to monopolize inheritance rights for the lawful children of an English aristocracy whose elders were often a philandering bunch and the frequent progenitors of out-of-wedlock offspring.

By the mid-20th century, the statute books of every state in the nation contained code sections creating, in varying but considerable detail, financial liabilities for people legally designated as illegitimates. On examination, these measures visibly served only the interests of insurance companies, pension funds, and other compensatory institutions looking for any excuse not to pay a claim.

Since then, public opinion has intelligently and compassionately rebelled against the practice of afflicting infants with the consequences of what may or may not have been their parents' indiscretions. As distaste for the bastardy classification evolved, it naturally began to be reflected legally. During the late 1960s, the United States Supreme Court established a strong record of striking down bastardy laws presented to it for evaluation. Arizona and Oregon have legislatively led the way toward eliminating the status altogether; hopefully, other states will soon follow.

Concurrently, the feminist progress of the past two decades has had a parallel effect of defusing most of the fears of being an unwed parent in America. For years, factions opposed to reunifications insisted that women who relinquished children born out of wedlock for adoption somehow needed protection from their pasts. Significantly, no comparable claim was ever made concerning unwed fathers. In a very condensed description, the popular attitude of the 1950s toward the unmarried family emphasizes stereotypes by which men could be strong and women could be victims.

Contemporary feminism has rendered that kind of thinking dangerous. At present, employers who let similar viewpoints affect their promotion policies would soon face lawsuits. Legislators who publicly espoused such positions could easily sow the seeds of their own defeat in a forthcoming election. Not unexpectedly, the same assertiveness that women now show professionally, politically, and in other ways, finds vivid expression in search circles. Birth mothers account for as much as a third of self-help organization membership. They bring tremendous resolve to research problems that are typically far more difficult, for reasons having to do with biases in record-keeping systems, than those posed to adult adoptees. They exhibit a very high degree of receptiveness when found.

Most of the credit for the strength and numbers of birth mothers in search rightfully belongs to the enduring women's rights struggle, which has captured wider attention and touched more lives than has its reunification counterpart. Self-help organizations, of course, provide their member birth mothers with moral support as well as technical advice. But their encouragement springs almost exclusively from feminist considerations. The women's movement has helped equip birth mothers to believe in themselves. Search and reunification is but one vehicle for exercising that belief.

As the processes of the sexual revolution and feminism took effect, they hastened yet another transformation of sorts that is at once highly favorable to searchers and deeply disturbing in its wider implications. They helped to redefine the psychological and sociological sciences in such a complete fashion that the behavioral scientists of all stripes who previously constituted the front line of resistance to reunifications lost most of their control over the activity.

During my brief tenure as a search counselor, I didn't have to listen to more than a few stories telling of visits to professional therapists who condemned reunifications efforts as "immoral" or "a sign of emotional imbalance" before I knew that I had heard too many. Their repetition was invariably dampening to my own spirits and those of the person with whom I was conversing.

Occasionally, other kinds of narratives were recounted. In these tales, therapists were in sympathy with the searcher's need to reconcile the past to the present. That in itself was not surprising. Under the plastic standards of the soft sciences, it is not unusual for two or more schools of thought to exist regarding the same subject. But subsequent research into the possible differences distinguishing the various groups on a range of issues including adoption, illegitimacy, unwed parenthood, and the like, resulted in two very unsettling discoveries.

First, after trudging for days through a university library's accumulation of more than 50 years of professional behavioral science journals, it became apparent that for all that time the most common concern of the psychologies and sociologies has been to reflect the public morality rather than to pursue and apply theraputically objective principles of human behavior. Over the decades, they have placed major emphasis on such goals as adjustment to social norms that in turn were a result of a meld of many influences including religion, politics, tradition and education. In other words, the soft sciences were often merely just one of the many cultural mechanisms available for the cultivation of mass conformity.

For behavioral scientists, from psychiatrists to masters of social work, that approach to their professional duties succeeded fairly well as long as the public morality remained somewhat stable. As a group, they could safely pronounce that a woman's place was in the home and a man's was in

24

> **"'I just want to know if he's all right, if he's happy. If I could just look at him one time and that's all he wanted, I would be content.'"**
> *—Birth mother speaking of her relinquished son, as quoted in the April 27, 1978*
> The Richmond News-Leader,
> *Richmond, Virginia*

business and politics. They opposed premarital sexual activity and unwed cohabitation. They claimed that adoptees who were properly raised would never want to know the facts of their origins.

But in the 1960s, the country's value systems changed drastically. The transformation occurred in such an open manner that there is no need to detail it here. In response, the behavioral sciences had to adapt quickly to a substantially different social situation. By 1965, a rising therapeutic career could not be based on comments such as those made on, say, the subject of illegitimacy by sociologist Kingsley Davis in the September 1939 *American Journal of Sociology*. In that magazine, Davis wrote:

> *"The bastard, like the prostitute, thief, and beggar, belongs to that motley crew of disreputable social types which society has generally resented, always endured. He is a living symbol of social irregularity, an undeniable evidence of contramoral forces..."*

No; by 1965, the behavioral scientists were well on their way toward reflecting the new popular consensus and confining what passes for their controversies to the limits set by the contemporary outlook. Bastards were not the only beneficiaries of the transition. At the time, to cite but two of many other examples of what was transpiring, four decades of attempts to establish that unwed mothers were typically of substandard intelligence were dropped, and unwed fathers began to be officially regarded as having an interest in their children. But as welcome as these changes were, as much as they alleviated the major pressures inhibiting search and reunification from becoming a widespread phenomenon, there is something disquieting about their method of arrival.

Throughout the 20th century, behavioral scientists have shown that they can command enormous influence over the lives of others. As personal counselors, they are invested with unusual trust and liberties to be inquisitive. They testify in court proceedings as expert witnesses. They appear at legislative hearings and influence governmental procedures. And yet, if their expertise is founded on an aptitude for echoing popular sentiments, then their scientific credentials are seriously flawed and important questions are raised concerning their ability to speak to adoptive issues at all.

Second, the trudge through 50 years of professional journals uncovered a partial answer to those questions: since the 1930s, behavioral scientists have repeatedly admitted in their writings that, with adoptive matters in general, they have been proceeding without proper factual and theoretical guidance. With often decisive, lasting effect on individual lives, they have been acting out of accepted practice rather than scientific principle. If these observations seem overly bold, consider the implications of the following material excerpted from a broad range of those publications:

"Many of those who sent replies referred to the fact that their answers were not based on a scientific accumulation of data; rather, they were personal reactions, 'hunches,' based on years of experience dealing with the problem."
"Suitability of The Child For Adoption"
American Journal of Orthopsychiatry
April 1937

"(O)ur work in the field of adoption, for all our legal, literary, and psychological manuscripts and our wordy records, is blind, slow, and stumbling."
"Adoption Procedure And The Community"

Mental Hygiene
April 1941

"(T)he philosophy of the particular social agency to whose attention she comes will to a large extent determine whether or not the unmarried mother will keep her baby."
"Problems of Illegitimacy as They Concern The Worker in The Field of Adoption"
Mental Hygiene
October 1941

"All workers in the field of adoptions wish they knew more about what has happened to the many children who have been adopted over the years. Obviously, much information is needed."
"Some Psychological Considerations in Adoption Practice"
Pediatrics
August 1957

"The failure to conduct research on unmarried fathers provides another illustration of how value dilemmas impede our understanding of illegitimacy. Only about one study of unmarried fathers exists for every 30 studies of unmarried mothers."
"Illegitimacy And Value Dilemmas"
The Christian Century
June 1963

"In adoption, as in other areas of social work and child welfare practice, a base of 'tested knowledge' and generally 'approved practice' is earnestly desired and sought. Yet in spite of extensive research activity and reporting of practice experience, little has been added to knowledge or practice theory in the past ten years that validates current practices or prescribes more effective ways of assuring desired outcomes."
"A New Look at Adoption: Current Development in The Philosophy And Practice of Adoption"
A Child Welfare League of America paper quoted in the book
Adoption—Is it for you?
1973

*"It is easy to forget whose baby it is and whose respon-
sibility it is to make all the little and the big decisions
about the baby. For instance, until recently there were two
hospitals in the Washington, D.C. area that refused an
unmarried mother the right to see her baby or get any information about him if the hospital knew she was thinking about relinquishing him for adoption—as if that were
the hospitals' right to give or withhold."*

"Unmarried Parenthood: Potential for Growth"
Adolescence
Summer 1974

*"The shift toward closed adoptions occurred in a
gradual, continuing pattern without critical evaluation of
the changes. There was no attempt to assess the
psychological burden of secrecy imposed upon adoptive
parents and adoptees, nor were the feelings of loss and
mourning by the birth parents carefully considered. It is
difficult to know why a process so final and irreversible as
the traditional relinquishment and adoption was so little
questioned by professionals in the field."*

"Open Adoption"
Social Work
March 1976

Given this list of admissions, which could run to much
greater length, the point is made. Behavioral scientists generally are in no position to address adoptive issues directly
and accurately. Unfortunately, that limitation has not historically prevented a sizable number of them from substituting
opinion for fact and exerting inordinate control over relin-
quishments, placements and reunifications. Traditionally, society has authorized therapists, counselors and caseworkers to
intervene in those procedures whether they knew what they
were doing or not.

By 1980, a substantial break with tradition has long been
under way. The sexual revolution eroded away many of the
behavioral scientists' prerogatives. The feminist movement of
the past two decades dissolved another fraction. The trend

> **"'You don't have to choose between two families,' she says today. 'You just have a bigger family.'"**
>
> *—Conclusion reached by a successful searcher, as reported in the November 19, 1978 San Francisco Sunday Examiner & Chronicle*

toward the acceptance of single parenthood took more. Then, well over 100,000 searchers arrived on the scene to press their own cause.

Now, rather than being allowed to act as one kind of guardian of public policy and popular morality, these professionals are being relegated to providing assistance in identifying problems, articulating feelings, and developing responses to both. That's probably how they should have been occupying their time all along. The change may be as healthy and welcome for them as it is for the adult adoptees and birth parents who become their clients.

So, for searchers as a group, the contrasts between Marilyn Monroe's 1951 and the present are vivid and encouraging. Now, a reunification effort finds greater support in the world. Its acceptance is based on better information pertaining to its whys and wherefores. Much of the opposition to the endeavor has faded. Finally, there is one remaining difference between the two periods that will be explored at length in the material to come: The current abundance of technical information detailing how a search is conducted.

SECTION I

You are about to turn yourself into an amateur detective. Within the boundaries of a reunification search, you will probably soon achieve more at the calling than most professionals. Private investigators for hire divide their time and talents among probes into such diverse irregularities as arson, illicit romances, industrial espionage, overdue child support, and insurance fraud. You have only one assignment, finding a missing person. The fact that you will be specializing works in your favor.

At the outset, it will help to know what your rights are in the situation. If you don't, people will occasionally mislead you on the subject. Some of them will merely be poorly informed; others will be deliberately attempting to frustrate your efforts. Regardless, under the circumstances, there are individual prerogatives that are legally protected either by the Constitution, by judicial acknowledgements, or by statute. For practical purposes, only two directly concern adult adoptees and birth parents: the right to search and the right of access to information.

As late as 1978, a few scattered news reports still characterized searches by adult adoptees and by birth parents of adult adoptees as illegal. They were wrong. To date, not a single law forbidding either searches or reunification has been entered anywhere in the combined civil and criminal codes of the federal government and the 50 states. As unprohibited activities, then, both theoretically benefit from certain constitutional guarantees derived under the theory of

31

liberties and the doctrine of familial rights that have evolved over years of United States Supreme Court history. Just how far these guarantees would extend in an actual conflict, however, is anybody's guess. The central constitutional issues of most adoptive controversies have yet to be litigated. Adult adoptees assuredly won't be arrested in the middle of records research (at least, nor for engaging in search activity). It is doubtful that they could employ the Constitution to force disclosure of the whereabouts of their brothers and sisters.

Birth parent searches for adopted, unemancipated minors, on the other hand, could easily run afoul of legal trouble. Adoptive parents are invested with the constitutional right to control their children's associations until their sons and daughters reach the age of majority. They would have many options in their response to a birth parent's arrival in their lives. If they chose to deny reunification contact with a minor under their care, any court of appropriate jurisdiction would likely support their decision with injunctions whose violation carried possible fines or imprisonment.

Confusion regarding the right to search stems primarily from the sealed records statutes whose application in most states concludes an adoption's finalization procedures. It has been assumed that a ban against searches was implied by their dictates. But what these measures do, and only do, is close adoption case files to subsequent examination, except by court order. Nothing is gained by reading more into them than is there.

Sealed records laws are also responsible for much of the muddled thinking in circulation regarding the right to access to information relevant to a search. Again, the problem is one of a broader interpretation of these acts than they deserve. An adoption case file represents only one source of the data needed to locate a birth relative. Ironically, most of the same data can be lawfully gathered elsewhere. Many searches are completed without a case file ever being cracked.

Where information gathering is legal, the prerogative is constitutionally protected as a right acknowledged by the United States Supreme Court. As such, it establishes a working relationship between the individual citizen and the government but does not go beyond into the private sector. The right of access to information does not automatically compel corporations, say, to allow outside inspection of their employee files.

With the government, the entitlement pertains most directly to an extensive range of material commonly described as "public record." In this category can be found probate files; birth, marriage and death certificates, voter registration affidavits, some government employment data, property assessment rolls, and the like. In practical terms highly encouraging to searchers, public record means that the government, through procedures compatible with effective storage and retrieval, must make this material available to any person on request.

Once adult adoptees and birth parents are secure in the knowledge of their legal rights, the detective work entailed by a search can be approached boldly. For many individuals, that security will at times serve as an invaluable source of comfort. If certain current reunification movement patterns continue to hold true, those occasions will usually arise in one of two circumstances. First, some of the nicest people, even close friends and relatives, will frequently attempt to persuade searchers away from their chosen task. Their advice is typically well intended and inevitably erroneous, a remaining vestige of the unhappy thinking that has historically surrounded adoptive matters. Second, searchers often find themselves unexpectedly taking a break from their endeavors. These pauses may last anywhere from a few weeks to a year or more and appear to be responses to the need to review events and to adjust to new feelings. But if unanticipated, they can be misinterpreted as resignation. In both instances, it may be reassuring to recall one's right to proceed at a pace of one's own determination.

The detective work will cost some money. I have yet to hear of anyone who has kept strict financial records of a search, but from many general accountings, it appears that outlays ranging from one hundred to four hundred dollars are not unusual. Phone bills, postage and transportation stand out as areas in which expenditures are customarily greatest. Scattered news reports tell of searches in which expenses ran as high as $3000. In each of those instances, private investigators had been retained and considerable professional fees had to be paid.

General preparation for a search can be completed in a few hours. The time is usually best spent alone, or possibly, in the company of a supportive intimate. It should be devoted to a review of everything you remember ever hearing over the years concerning your personal background as an adoptee or as a birth parent who has relinquished a child for adoption.

The review could result in considerable information. For adoptees, the list of details, if any, may includes: when you parents first told you of your adoption; your original cultural history; whether a placement agency, a physician, or an attorney handled your adoption; your birth parents' approximate ages when they relinquished you, the possible reasons for relinquishment; the state, county and hospital in which you were born; and so on. For birth parents: the name of the facility in which the child was born, the delivery doctor's name, the name of the agency or party to whom the child was relinquished, anything you may have been told about the prospective adoptive parents, the amount and nature of any possible social welfare benefits received during pregnancy, and the like.

The particulars should be entered in a notebook or journal that can be used to chronicle search strategies and developments. It is important to write down for safekeeping every detail that can be rescued from the past no matter how slight and unimaginative it may appear. If properly evaluated, any of these items may constitute a valuable lead.

Not unexpectedly, the actual sleuthing chores will turn out to be very easy for some and exceptionally difficult for others. One woman of my acquaintance discovered a previously unknown sister in a surprisingly brief three days. Another devoted more than 20 years to locating her mother.

On the average, however, adult adoptees will spend two to

> "A group of Oklahoma adoptees, who claim they are kept strangers to their past by antiquated state laws, is planning to push for legislative reforms at a Thursday committee hearing at the state Capitol.
>
> "The object of the renewed lobbying effort is a bill that would give adoptees a greater opportunity to discover their true identities through legal records that are kept sealed under current state law."
>
> —*From the June 21, 1978*
> *Oklahoma City, Oklahoma* Times

three years of occasional lunch hours, evenings, and weekends completing their searches. The factors influencing that average are numerous. They include the information practices laws of the state or states in which a sought-after relative has resided, the adoptive placement laws of the jurisdiction in which an adoption was finalized, searchers' ages when they begin their investigatory activities and the personal hours available for research.

The variables apparently only influence a search's duration. With the exception of circumstances in which a birth relative is deceased, they seem to have little bearing on the eventual conclusion of the endeavor. The completion rates reported by the reunification movement run extremely high. If they constitute a proper measure, once a concrete decision to embark is made, it seems almost inevitable that parent and offspring will one day meet.

For birth parents, the time needed for completion of a search is usually much longer. There are exceptions.

Occasionally an individual's birth parents and adoptive parents know one another personally and are on appreciably friendly terms. Then, no real detective problems exist. But from the viewpoint of most birth parents, a relinquished child disappears for at least 18 years into a new identity that can't even be guessed at for any practical purpose. Normally, few if any traces of the youngster are left behind. In contrast, at the time of relinquishment, most birth parents are of an age when many details of their lives have already been entered into the directories and files that are the stuff of searches. From then to the present, they leave a running trail of clues to their whereabouts in city directories, health department archives, church registries, and elsewhere. As a result, adult adoptee searches for birth parents are generally far easier than the converse birth parent searches for adult adoptees.

The forthcoming technical information reflects that advantage. It is oriented to address the needs of adult adoptees first and those of birth parents second. Political as well as practical considerations underlie this approach. Obviously, if the chances of success favor one group over the other, attempts should be made to take advantage of those odds. During the 1980's, institutional resistance to reunifications is likely to be overcome by the simple fact of numbers. As success comes to the current searching thousands the bureaucratic arguments against their activities will progressively weaken. With resistance fading, the way becomes ever easier for all subsequent searchers, adoptees and birth parents alike. When a head count makes the difference, that's politics. And in this political situation, there's a point to using technical information to increase the number of people in the head count as swiftly as possible.

Searching birth parents will find much that is helpful in the following material. But now, the lead goes to adult adoptees. Their next step is to obtain a copy of the amended birth certificate, modified to carry the names and home addresses of adoptive parents, that was typically issued for each of them after their adoptions were finalized. There is no legal way that this document can be withheld from an adult for whom it was originally issued, so no intractable problems should arise here.

Adoptive parents frequently have a copy of the amended birth certificate among their personal papers. Most are willing to pass it along. If they don't have a copy, a certificate can be acquired from the birth records department of the county in which an adoptee was born, for a fee running to no more than $3.00 in most jurisdictions. If the county is unknown, a letter of inquiry to an appropriate state agency should turn up either the document, which will be duplicated and forwarded for similarly nominal fees, or directions leading to its whereabouts. The letter should contain an adoptee's name, birth date, and request for a records search. In the western states, those agencies include:

Alaska

Bureau of Vital Statistics
Pouch H
Juneau, 99801

Arizona

Division of Vital Records
Department of Health
P.O. Box 3887
Phoenix, 85030

California

State Department of Public Health
Bureau of Vital Statistics
410 N Street
Sacramento, 95814

Hawaii

Research and Statistics Office
State Department of Health
P.O. Box 3378
Honolulu, 96801

Idaho

Bureau of Vital Statistics
  Department of Environmental Protection and Health
  State House
  Boise, 83720

Nevada

Division of Vital Statistics
  Department of Health, Welfare and Rehabilitation
  Division of Health
  Carson City, 89710

Oregon

Statistics Section
  State Board of Health
  P.O. Box 231
  Portland, 97207

Washington

State Department of Health
  Bureau of Vital Statistics
  P.O. Box 709
  Olympia, 98504

If the state in which a searching adoptee was born is un-known, then letters to every appropriate state agency in the country become necessary. A list of those agencies and their addresses is available in a federal Department of Health, Education and Welfare publication titled "Where To Write for Birth and Death Records." The pamphlet can be purchased for 35 cents at the federal bookstore nearest you, or for $1.00, because of minimum mail order requirements, from the U.S. Government Printing Office, Washington, D.C. 20402. It should be referred to by its stock number, 017-022-00486-1.

If a mass mailing of that sort fails to turn up anything, then the services of a professional investigator become advisable.

The information entered onto a birth certificate varies con-siderably from state to state. At minimum, it will ordinarily verify an adoptee's birth date, which is important as one of the few concrete, biographical details known to both birth mothers and their offspring. Elsewhere, the document is more generous in its holdings. In California, for one, it often contains the name of the hospital in which a person was born and the name of the doctor who attended the delivery. Those particulars are valuable clues and they remain unchanged on amended certificates.

On very rare occasions, such as with babies abandoned shortly after delivery, the certificate will carry only an estimated birth date. That circumstance clearly inhibits a search's progress; it does not preclude reunification.

With or without an amended birth certificate on hand, adult adoptees can begin looking for the single most valuable piece of information they will pursue throughout the course of a search: a birth parent's name. Certain opportunities to uncover that item won't open up until the document arrives. Its absence does not provide cause for delay. Ordinarily, there are seven possible sources from which a birth parent's name can surface: adoptive parents, delivery doctors, hospital birth records, church registries, newspaper vital statistics announcements, unamended birth certificates and other documents freed from sealed records files, and newspaper advertising. Which of the seven a searcher wishes to turn to first is primarily a matter of where he or she feels most comfortable. In working terms, each of the seven looks something like this:

ADOPTIVE PARENTS

To date, no reliable measures exist as to the attitudes and feelings that adoptive parents as a group hold toward reunifications. Articles in a few behavioral science journals have suggested that they invariably look upon the practice with some dismay. Yet, scattered news reports from around the country reveal that adoptive parents often participate actively in searches.

The news reports may indicate a trend. For some 40 to 50

years, adoptive parents, much like birth parents, have been overly subject to the influence exerted by public and private placement agency caseworkers who have traditionally opposed renewed contact between birth parents and their relinquished offspring. Today that influence has waned. Now, adoptive parents are undoubtedly much more inclined to resolve with their sons and daughters any conflicts that prospective reunifications might arouse. Once the conflicts are settled, a search can become a family affair.

If such a trend is underway, it can only be opportune. In addition to the moral support they can provide—even as an adult, there's often nothing like having mom and dad in your corner—adoptive parents frequently are in possession of far more information regarding an adoptee's biological history than is popularly assumed. Alternatively, they may have a very good idea of where the pertinent names and dates can be found.

Parental access to information stems from the fact that American adoptions are implemented in more than one fashion. The full number of them are divided by statisticians into two roughly equal classifications popularly referred to as "relative" and "nonrelative" adoptions. The first category is for the most part defined by stepparents adopting a spouse's child by a previous marriage. The formalities are customarily simple and direct. There is also no mystery here as to the identity of the relinquishing parent, should the adoptee ever want to know. In a nonrelative adoption, neither parent is genetically related to the child. The procedures are technically more complex. They require more paperwork.

Roughly 50 percent of all nonrelative adoptions are completed outside of placement agency auspices in what is commonly described as an "independent" or "private placement" adoption. With these, the parents often retain the file of official papers that is normally sealed and withheld by placement agencies after an adoption's finalization. The papers, with rare exceptions, typically contain names and other leads of major importance to searching adoptees. Alternatively, the material frequently remains in the keeping of the attorney who assisted the parents in the proceedings.

Finally, through a slip of the tongue or some other fluke, even placement agency caseworkers occasionally reveal to adopting couples some detail that may prove useful to inquiring minds some years later. So regardless of whether a person was placed in a relative or nonrelative, independent or agency adoption, enlistment of parental support at the outset is a good way to advance a search.

DELIVERY DOCTORS

State boards of medical examiners or medical quality assurance, as their names imply, are regulatory commissions charged with the responsibility of providing the public with minimal guarantees as to the competence and good standing of doctors practicing within their attendant jurisdictions. As part of their routine duties, these boards will supply on request the office address of any physician under their authority.

The boards' address services may allow searchers to locate the doctors who delivered them at birth. This is especially true for adoptees who embark on a quest for their birth parents during the initial years of adulthood, say, between the ages of 18 and 25. For them, the likelihood is strong that the pertinent physicians have not yet reached retirement age and so are still active in their profession. Once contacted, the doctors, according to their understanding of the ethics of the situation, will often share what they have on record and in memory of a searching adoptee's personal history, including the names of his or her birth parents.

Of course, for searchers residing in the same area in which they were born, the doctor's office address may be no further away than the yellow pages of their local phone book. When luck breaks like that, communication with the state board can be skipped entirely. Otherwise, here are the procedural specifics:

To respond at all, the medical board of the state in which a searching adoptee was born will need the name of the physician being sought. Hopefully, that particular item will have been discovered as an entry on a birth certificate or in an adoption records file. It can also, at times, be found in a collection of prenatal and natal documents known as a "Record of Birth," which will be explained at length below.

But assuming that the doctor's name has been unearthed, then the board's job of geographic location should encounter no difficulties whatsoever. The service is so simple that, to date, no fees are connected with it. The entire transaction can be conducted through the mails by forwarding a letter of inquiry to the appropriate following address:

Alaska

Board of Medical Examiners
   Department of Commerce and Economic Development
   Division of Occupational Licensing

Pouch H
Juneau, 99801

Arizona

Board of Medical Examiners
810 West Bethany Home Road
Phoenix, 85013

California

Board of Medical Quality Assurance
1430 Howe Avenue
Sacramento, 95825

Hawaii

Department of Regulatory Agencies
Licensing Division, Medicine
P.O. Box 3469
Honolulu, 96801

Idaho

Board of Medicine
P.O. Box 6817
Boise, 83707

Nevada

Board of Medical Examiners
P.O. Box 7238
Reno, 89510

Oregon

Board of Medical Examiners
1002 Loyalty Building
317 Southwest Alder
Portland, 97204

Washington

Board of Medical Examiners
Division of Professional Licensing
P.O. Box 9649
Olympia, 98504

Birth Parent Addendum: In almost all instances, a delivery doctor who knows that a birth mother wishes to be found will naturally be more inclined to respond favorably to a searching adult adoptee's request for her name and other information leading to her whereabouts. Any birth mother who desires an eventual reunification, then, should also locate the doctor who attended to her relinquished offspring's arrival into the world and advise that physician, either by letter or in personal conversation, of her preferences in the matter. By including a current address in her communication, a birth mother may establish for a searcher a direct route from the doctor's office to her front door.

HOSPITAL BIRTH RECORDS

When a person is born in a hospital, as most of us were, the facility is required by law to retain some record of the event. This material is customarily referred to as a "Record of Birth." It is comprised of originals or copies of the several documents compiled by physicians who attend to mothers' health needs from the onset of pregnancy through delivery. Included in the compilation are forms attesting to compliance with legal essentials such as the placement of antiblindness drops in an infant's eyes. Other entries are exclusively medical in nature.

Many hospitals, as a matter of standard operating procedure, will continue to store birth records long after they would have been disposed of by most private practitioners. As might be expected from their description, these papers can often supply search information in generous measure, particularly a mother's name, age, and home address at the time of a relinquished individual's birth. They may even provide a fact or two concerning the purported father.

But for all that, certain frustrating problems are commonly associated with the attempted retrieval and use of birth records to further a search. The forms and documents are at times only indirectly available to adult adoptees. The data contained in them are not always accurate. Here's the full story:

Under California law, which in this matter is roughly

comparable to law prevalent in other western states, licensed hospitals are obligated to keep patient records active and accessible for a minimum of seven years or, with minors, until one year after a patient reaches legal adulthood. In regulatory terms, a newborn baby is regarded as a patient.

After the minimum required time, patient files may be destroyed when and as an institution sees fit. But if it suits a facility's purposes, these materials may be stored indefinitely. Research centers, for example, regard medical records as an invaluable resource for studying the long-term effects of various treatment regimens. At the warehouses of the University of California San Francisco Medical Center, to name one, case histories can be traced back as far as the late 1800s.

To stand any chance at all of gaining entrance to a record of birth, a searcher will have to be in possession of the surname he or she was born under. Persons adopted after the age of three or four frequently remember that detail firsthand. Otherwise, it can hopefully be supplied by an adoptive parent, from an adoption records file, or from other sources mentioned in this section.

The name of the facility in which a person was born is occasionally found on an amended birth certificate. If it is not entered there, and searchers know both their original surnames and the general geographic area of their birth, then a round of inquiring telephone calls to that region's hospitals may turn up something—provided, of course, those hospitals hold on to the appropriate records for a sufficient length of time. If neither recourse works, then the appeal again has to be made to adoptive parents and adoption records files.

The operating procedures governing access to personal medical records vary only slightly among institutions. Each must be presented with a letter authorizing the release of the material and specifying to whom it is to be sent. The correspondence must also include a searcher's birth date and original surname for hospital personnel to key the request into their filing systems.

But assuming that searchers have located hospitals in possession of the desired documents and have provided them with the necessary specifics, there is still a catch. Some hospitals will forward medical records to the person asking for them, but others will send the material only to an individual's private physician. In the latter instance, obviously, it is crucial for adult adoptees to be working in conjunction with a sympathetic doctor.

Copying fees may be charged for duplication of birth records. They usually run to no more than 50 cents per page.

Finally, to avoid bitter disappointment, it should be remembered that under the cruel pressures of yesteryear, unwed mothers frequently used fictitious names upon admission to delivery wards. The odds are good that the birth mother's name found in a record of birth is a true one. But they are not 100 percent.

Birth Parent Addendum: Here, too, birth mothers have the opportunity to help the search process along by forwarding to the records departments of the hospitals in which their relinquished offspring were born, letters authorizing the release of personal medical-file information to all inquirers.

CHURCH REGISTRIES

Church registries are ecclesiastical ledgers into which are entered information pertaining to an individual's reception of the sacred rites. Apparently all Christian denominations maintain such records and, probably, every other religious body whose practices embrace periodic observances amounting to sacraments or their equivalent does likewise. In the Judaic tradition, the chronicle entries begin either with the rite of circumcision or with an infant-naming ceremony.

Christian registries, which for purely numerical reasons will be of the most interest to searchers as a group, are generally organized first by sacrament and then by date. The method reflects the fact that in as highly a mobile society as ours, specific rites may be administered at widely differing times and geographic locations in a believer's life, rendering impractical any filing system keyed to names. Consistent with that approach, the commonly kept ledgers include marriage registries, communion registries, and those godsends to inquiring adult adoptees, baptismal registries.

The information contained in a baptismal registry entry ordinarily includes the original given name and surname of the person being baptized, the name of one or both birth parents, and the names of the godparents, if any. By virtue of being born into a largely Christian society, most adoptees received a Christian baptism shortly after birth. At the time, they were often still in the custody of their birth mothers, at least, and therefore the registry marking the occasion is likely to contain names and other personal details of major importance to them.

The name and location of the church at which a baptism was administered should be available for the asking because certain religious imperatives exist to impel placement agencies or parents to advise adoptees of where they received the sacrament. Roman Catholicism, for one, requires a recent verification of baptism and Holy Communion before its priests will officiate at a formal church wedding. Some similar rule undoubtedly holds true for most Christian faiths. If a particular parish has gone out of existence, which happens on rare occasions, its registries will be held by its denominational headquarters.

Entrance to baptismal registries is governed by canon law, rather than civil, which seems to defer to local parish policies on the matter. To date, no reports of searchers being denied access to this material have surfaced, although each local church seems to have its own procedural preferences in the matter. On my rounds, I stopped at the Roman Catholic Our Lady of The Visitation. There, the rectory staff sat me down with the proper ledger and busied themselves elsewhere while I flipped pages. San Francisco's Episcopal diocesan office, on the other hand, advised me over the phone that it would prefer a letter of inquiry containing the approximate date of the baptism. With that, I was told, its own personnel would conduct the research and then reply.

At present, no fees are connected with any religious registry research services.

NEWSPAPER VITAL STATISTICS ANNOUNCEMENTS

Under the heading "Vital Statistics," or its equivalent, most newspapers regularly publish listings of recent births, deaths, marriages, and divorces occurring in the community the publication serves. The birth announcements are customarily accompanied by the parents' names. It follows, then, that specific back issues of certain newspapers are of major interest to searching adoptees.

The problem, of course, is how a searcher currently residing in Spokane, but who was born in Los Angeles, gets a look at, say, a copy of the June 20, 1946 *Herald-Tribune*. The solution is microfilm or, as it is otherwise known, microform.

The Library of Congress reference volume titled *Newspapers On Microform* is comprised of little more than an extensive listing of approximately 34,000 daily and weekly newspapers whose entire chronological contents, as they were available, have been photographed onto reels of microfilm for purposes of preservation, efficient storage, and research. Through a national Interlibrary Loan System, any one of these reels can find its way to almost any public or private library in the country.

As described by a San Francisco librarian, the loan process is normally quite simple. Library membership is generally a prerequisite. To cover postage costs, service fees ranging from 25 to 50 cents per reel are usually necessary. Once ordered, reels take from one to two months to arrive. They can be held for two weeks. Almost every library in the country today owns at least one projection device on which the microfilm can be screened.

Unfortunately, the San Francisco librarian was the third in as many libraries who I had approached on the subject. The previous two professed to know of this interlibrary system. So searchers who go this route may have to educate people along the way. To help with that eventuality, a copy of the standard loan request form is included in this book's appendix.

> "In Kansas, which has been issuing original birth certificates to adult adoptees since 1951, Barbara J. Sabol, director of services to children and youth, knows of only one 'negative reaction' to a reunion.
>
> "Though there have been disappointments, she reports, 'all who were asked about reunions report feeling better about themselves because they have had answers to their questions.'".
>
> —*From the July 19, 1978 San Antonio, Texas* Express

After an appropriate vital statistics section is identified, a few problems arise. In years past, notice of out-of-wedlock births was typically withheld from the public. But they do not all go unheralded and not every adoptee was so born. In addition, even if listed, birth parents' names will not always be immediately recognizable. They would stand out if already known, but then, there would be no need for the microfilm in the first place. The best searchers can usually do here is to record all the adult names accompanying the birth of a child of their own gender and begin tracing each down. For many, that's an effective start.

A list of major western states libraries is also included in this book's appendix.

SEALED RECORDS FILES

Why all but two state legislatures ever passed sealed records laws in the first place is something of a continuing mystery. There is no ready evidence to establish that these statutes have contributed anything positive to the institution of adoption in America. Nor has adoption appeared to suffer in jurisdictions without them, which at present are only Alabama and Kansas. In those two states, searchers may gain admittance to their adoption files simply by asking for them at the civic office in which the material is stored.

Nonetheless, essentially equivalent sealed records statutes now exist in 48 states. Each of these measures allows the contents of an adoption file to be unsealed and disclosed by order of the court of appropriate jurisdiction. Because a file's enclosed papers can characteristically provide crucial search information to adult adoptees, it is usually worth expending whatever effort is necessary to obtain the appropriate court order.

Typically, a plea to open sealed records is decided upon by a lower court presiding in the county in which a person was adopted. A county clerk of the same municipality can identify the proper bench exactly. To act, the court must be presented with a formal petition, which is usually comprised of a completed and notarized civil form, available also from the county clerk, accompanied by as much supportive material as possible. In California, at least, county clerks will occasionally deny the existence of the petition form. Resistance to searches can pop up anywhere. Don't believe them.

The judge will generally rule on the petition in his or her private chambers. The proceeding is not one for open court. In reaching a decision, the bench is lawfully entitled to consider a wide variety of factors including pressing needs for medical information, the emotional imperatives underlying a search, adoptive parent endorsement of the activity, and the like.

Whether a lawyer's services are at all helpful in this action is anybody's guess. There are as many reports in circulation of petitions granted without an attorney's help as with it. However, what is indisputedly important is that a searcher provide the court with as much succinct, supportive material as can be generated. Medical claims should be verified by a physician corresponding on professional stationery. Statements of personal emotional needs should be precise, complete, and candid. Any judicial request for additional information should be responded to quickly and thoroughly.

In recent years, courts have become increasingly sympathetic toward petitions of this nature. A few have even concluded that the searcher's need to know about his or her past alone provides sufficient good cause to warrant opening sealed records. Over the next decade, that receptiveness may come to predominate in judicial opinion.

NEWSPAPER ADVERTISING

This is admittedly a long shot. It's been known to work. Two facts that are very important to searches are usually known to both a birth mother and her relinquished offspring: the latter's gender and birth date. With those details, it is possible for a searching adoptee to make contact with a birth mother through a brief message inserted in the "Personals" or "Announcements" columns of a newspaper's classified advertising section.

The ad can follow this approximate form:

"(Male/female) adult adoptee born (insert date) seeks any and all information regarding birth mother. Reply to (insert address and/or phone number)."

There are additional bits of information that, if known, should appear in the ad. These may include an adoptee's place of birth, the name of the agency to which he or she was relinquished, and an original religious affiliation.

Obviously, this technique can be equally opportune for searching birth mothers. Their ad should read something like this:

"Birth mother of (male/female) adoptee born (insert date) seeks any and all information regarding offspring's whereabouts. Reply to (insert address and/or phone number)."

These ads should first appear in the specific region, and then throughout the state, where an adoptee was born. Costs for classified advertising vary considerably between newspapers but a figure of about $12.00 for three lines of copy published for a one week run is not uncommon.

SECTION II

Once a name has been obtained, the world's considerable weight shifts onto a searcher's side. Much of the advantage gained is in terms of procedural benefits. As one example of the shift's effects, many informational resources of interest to inquiring adoptees require names in order to become operative. These resources are extraordinarily diverse and range anywhere from reference books on library shelves to various government files organized and housed in municipal offices and warehouses. Continuing on, much of the pertinent material stored by the government is officially classified as "public record." When a person requests public record information, access to it must be given to him or her as a matter of law. A name, then, opens up new research possibilities while foreclosing some of society's options to say "no" to a searcher.

But in addition, many people who are reluctant to divulge search-related data appear to focus their hesitations on the name of the person being sought. When approached, they become much more relaxed after learning that they are not going to be asked to disclose an appellation. They also seem to assume that if a name has been acquired, then there is little point in withholding anything else.

The assumption is for the most part correct. A search is possible because we reside in a society possessed by an insatiable hunger for gathering and absorbing information about its constituent members. From birth, and in the public sector and the private, details of our lives are constantly dated, located, registered, recorded and reviewed. As the United

States advances toward the 21st century, it has become exceedingly difficult, if not impossible, for an individual to lead a normal life without being converted into an entry in a large number of economic, academic and legal files. Whether that's ultimately good or bad for the nation and its citizens is a problem for philosophers to ponder. At the moment, though, it's terrific for searchers.

In their proper sequence, the entries constitute a faint trail by which a person's life is traceable from its earliest days to the present. The inquiring adult adoptee's next job, then, is to find passage onto that trail. For all practical purposes, the path can be picked up anywhere. So long as an individual is geographically placed somewhere in the past, he or she can usually be tracked forward through the years with relative ease. The route can be identified by the discovery of a specific address where a birth relative once resided.

On trail, events can move very swiftly. Already a few slim chances exist that a search's completion will be precipitated by the uncovering of a name alone. If adoptive parents originally knew the birth parents, they may be able to help establish an immediate connection. A delivery doctor may still be a birth mother's personal physician. If a name appears in response to newspaper classified advertising, the respondent will likely be the person being sought.

An address vastly increases the number of possibilities. It can reduce the time needed to finish a search from months to minutes. Obviously, it is a detail second only to a name in importance. For adult adoptees, the pursuit of addresses should ideally begin in the town or city where they were born. From there, the item will generally turn up in one of six possible sources: Telephone directories, city directories, state vital statistics offices, probate records, voter registration affidavits, and motor vehicle department records. In working terms, each looks something like this:

TELEPHONE DIRECTORIES

The national Bell System's full set of telephone directories apparently constitutes the single most complete listing available for public inspection of the names, addresses, and, of course, phone numbers of the country's individual citizens. Naturally, that means something to a reunification effort. Both current and back issues of these directories can be used to complete a search.

On rare occasion, birth relatives have been located by an extended browse through the entire country's telephone books. The job is awesomely tedious, but then nobody every said a search would always be exciting. These volumes can generally be found in two places. In most major metropolitan areas, at least one Bell System branch office provides public access to all or most current United States phone directories as well as to those of a fair number of foreign provinces and cities. In addition, smaller but similar collections are housed by many county public library systems in their central facilities, along with directory back issues of the community served by the library.

But generally, however, a browse won't be sufficient to make the desired connection. What might work, however, is a mass mailing of a letter of inquiry to every person in the country, and perhaps to points beyond, bearing a surname identical to that of the person being sought. For such a mailing, there is no better source of addresses than the Bell System's directories. True, if a birth relative's last name is Smith or Jones, the task will be enormous. But for committed searchers, sometimes there is no other choice. To help with the task, an example of a possible letter of inquiry is included in this book's appendix.

This technique has its evident variations and problems. If a birth relative's full name is known, letters can be limited to people of similar given names and first initials and duplicate last names. On the other hand, I had a full name when I sat down to look for a half-brother who had not been relinquished for adoption. I persevered through every phone book in the country. I posted my letters. I later discovered that my brother has an unlisted phone number. Sometimes, that's just the way it goes.

Back issues of telephone directories present a different kind of opportunity. A phone book two or three decades old may provide an address suitable for following a person into the present. The ways in which that detail can be effective utilized are described at length in forthcoming sections of this book titled "Assessor's Office," "Knocking On Neighborhood Doors," and "Social Security Administration."

CITY DIRECTORIES

City directories were a late discovery for me. I first learned of their existence more than a year after I found my birth father, deceased, and several months after successfully connecting with my birth mother. Had I known about them at the outset of my endeavors, my 10 months of sleuthing would have been reduced to about 10 days. In one volume's pages is listed the home address of the half-brother who was absent from the phone book.

City directories are thick and marvelous reference works intended to be of principal value to business and industry. They are commonly referred to as Caron, Hill, Polk, or Williams directories. These and other titles each reflect the name of a particular publisher. It appears that R.L. Polk & Co. of Dallas, Texas is the largest producer of these tomes. The corporation claims to print more than 1400 editions of its product.

Polk directories, then, can be considered representative of the genre. Locked into a single style, they are divided into four sections, the second and third of which are of major relevance to searchers.

Section two gathers together the names of every person, business firm, and corporation within a city and lists them alphabetically along with each individual's marital status, occupation, and address, and with each commercial operation's nature, address, and official personnel.

In section three, all of a community's streets and address numbers are entered in an equally well-organized fashion. With every entry appears the names and telephone numbers—excluding those that are also unlisted in standard telephone books—of either the business established at that location or of all persons residing there.

> "When we left to go back to Virginia, we stopped at the court house and I went in by myself this time. I asked for my file and it seemed like the woman was gone an hour. She was very ugly to me when she came back. She began to lecture me on how I should go on without finding out.
>
> "'I'm not a very rash person. I don't make waves, scream or stomp, but I got very ugly. I demanded to see her supervisor. Finally she gave me my records.'"
>
> —*From the April 28, 1978*
> The Richmond News Leader, *Richmond, Virginia*

Searching adult adoptees who locate an address in section two should immediately cross-refer the information to section three in an effort to discover if any other persons were residing at that street number at the time. In directories 20 to 30 years old, additional names found in section three may belong to an adoptee's birth grandparents.

Commercial demand for city directories is limited. As a result, they are very expensive to buy. They are normally purchased only by the business community and are not widely circulated. Major county, suburban, and metropolitan libraries, however, will frequently stock them. A state capital library will typically amass directories for the areas of the state for which they have been issued. Any given facility's collection may also include volumes for significant urban areas throughout the country and local back issues running into the past for a century or more.

Further use of the data found in city directories will be detailed in subsequent sections of this book titled "Probate Records," "Assessor's Office," "Professional Directories," "Knocking On Neighborhood Doors," and "Social Security Administration."

VITAL STATISTICS OFFICES

An essential part of every state government is a documentation office responsible for gathering, organizing and making public details pertaining to births, marriages and deaths that have occurred within their jurisdictions. Known generally by titles that include the words "vital statistics," these bureaus conduct their main business through systems of certificate storage and retrieval. On the certificates is customarily imprinted a generous measure of potentially valuable search information.

A fully completed marriage certificate may contain any and all of the following items: The names, ages, and residences of the bride and groom at the time of their wedding; their respective birth dates, and the name of the state or country in which each was born. It may also carry the names of the newlyweds' fathers, their mothers' maiden names, and the marriage witnesses' names.

The material entered onto a death certificate may include the deceased's birth date, social security number, and home address at the time of death; the names and birth places of the departed's parents; the name and occupation of his or her spouse, if any; and the name of the person reporting the death.

Birth certificates have been previously described in section one of this book. Current addresses for vital statistics offices in western states are also listed there.

A copy of a marriage or death certificate can ordinarily be readily obtained by forwarding a letter of request and a two-or-three-dollar records search and copying fee to the appropriate vital statistics bureau. The correspondence is best if kept brief. It should indicate what type of copied certificate is desired as well as the exact or approximate date on which the certified event took place. It should also include as much background material as is known regarding the person for whom the certificate was written.

At minimum, an identifying name and the approximate date of the event are usually needed by a bureau to respond affirmatively to a certificate copy request. If an approximate date is not available, some offices have been known to proceed successfully from a year when a person was last known to be single or alive.

PROBATE RECORDS

Probate records are civil documents relating to the final affairs of deceased persons, dealing either with the execution and administration of wills or with the disposal of remaining personal assets under circumstances in which no will was left or discovered.

These documents fall within the legal boundaries of public record. They are accessible to all inquiring parties through the county clerk's office of the jurisdiction in which the deceased passed away. They contain such details as the names and addresses of survivors informed of the death. These are usually next of kin, intimate friends, and other persons with a legitimate interest in the estate.

Most probate files of interest to searching adoptees will be those of their birth grandparents, since for the most part their birth parents are still alive. So far, the grandparents' identities may have been revealed by adoptive parents, by a delivery doctor, by an old telephone or city directory, or by a birth parent's marriage certificate. If their names have surfaced, attempts should be made to determine if they are still counted among the living and can be contacted personally. That task might call for as much as another complete browse through all the country's telephone books and another mass mailing.

Of course, nothing may turn up. Then it will become advisable to write to the vital statistics office of the state in which a grandparent was last known to reside for a possible death certificate. A copy in the return mail will be conclusive. The home address entered onto it will indicate the civil jurisdiction in which possible probate records are filed.

Once the preliminaries have been completed, the remaining steps in probate record research are blandly procedural. The address of a county clerk's office is regularly listed in the white pages of a community telephone book under the general heading of county government offices. Within the department, the probate section is always clearly demarcated. The personnel assigned there are generally pleasantly cooperative.

To respond to a request for a file, probate personnel must be presented with the case number under which the relevant probate actions were originally taken. This number is available from large index volumes commonly known as "Probate Indices" that are normally shelved immediately outside the section service counter for ease of handling.

The indices are usually organized first by intervals of time. In San Francisco, for example, they are arranged in 15 year periods. They are then subordered alphabetically, much after the fashion of encyclopedias. Hence, the requirements are the name of the deceased grandparent and, as near as possible, the date of death. The entries inside the indices, however, are sent down in only *approximate* alphabetical order and as a result must be reviewed with care.

Not every death is followed by a probate action. But for those that are, a cautious scan of the timely probate index will turn up the proper case number. Given that number, a probate clerk will be able to produce a desired file in a matter of minutes if a death was of fairly recent occurrence. If the decease took place some years in the past, the probate records are likely to be stored outside the county clerk's office and may require from 24 to 48 hours for their retrieval.

At present, no fees are connected with this service. Most county clerk's offices provide table or desk space at which probate files may be examined leisurely.

VOTER REGISTRATION AFFIDAVITS

In the United States, the exercise of the right to vote carries with it the purely procedural necessity of adding one's name to the civic voter registration rolls. This requirement is fulfilled by filing a simple form with the government attesting to one's qualification by age and citizenship to vote and avowing that one is not encumbered by an legal penalty that would inhibit the franchise. Officially titled an "Affidavit of Registration" this document is on some occasions of value to searchers.

The occasions are few. Under most circumstances, when a birth relative has been located sufficiently enough to reveal where he or she is likely to vote, the municipal store of affidavits is low on the list of source material that a searching adoptee should scan for specific addresses. A thumb through a local telephone book or city directory would likely prove more productive.

But it is always possible that a birth relative has an unlisted phone number or has withheld consent for entry into a city directory. The voter rolls may then supply information unavailable elsewhere. The pertinent data may be found on either current or canceled affidavits. To the specifics:

Voter registration ordinarily takes place in the county of a person's residence. Within certain limits, state election codes commonly allow individual counties to determine the look and final content of the voter registration forms used in their particular jurisdictions.

When properly and fully completed, the details found on the forms invariably include a voter's name, address and occupation at the time of registration, his or her birth date, state or country of birth, and a declaration of party affiliation, if any. But in, say, parts of Nevada, if a registrant has a social security number, its entry on the affidavit is mandatory, whereas in parts of California, its inclusion is optional.

A registration is permanent for life unless canceled for one of several reasons. These include the failure to vote in certain elections, a change of residence followed by re-registration elsewhere, cancellation at a voter's request (which occurs most often with a switch in party affiliation), the legal establishment of a registrant's insanity, and conviction for an infamous crime.

In one of many measures taken to inhibit voter fraud, registration affidavits have been statutorily classified as public record. They may be examined, for any reason whatsoever, by losing candidates, reporters, and other interested parties including searching adult adoptees and birth parents. The forms are usually organized and stored by a county office designated by an appreciably obvious title such as "Registrar of Voters" or "Elections Commission." The correct office can be located exactly through the central telephone switchboard of any county government's municipal offices.

Most state elections codes allow affidavits to be gathered into any orderly arrangement prescribed by a local county clerk. They also similarly stipulate that the clerk shall provide, to use California's wording, "for general use in his office, a comprehensive, printed alphabetical index to the surnames on all uncanceled affidavits for the whole of the county, whereby the affidavit of registration of any voter may be ascertained and produced."

It is to that index that searching adult adoptees must first turn if they are to make use of voter registration affidavits. There, the alphabetical listing of surnames will be keyed to the registrant's precinct number. The number will be duplicated on one of the full set of precinct files also housed in this government office. The files are typically a series of trays into which all current affidavits within a precinct are entered alphabetically. Research among them may be conducted with or without a clerk's assistance, depending on local procedural preferences.

In a few jurisdictions, counties will exercise their prerogative to go beyond an elections code's miminum stipulations by printing affidavits in two sizes, a larger for most general purposes and smaller for registration by mail. These are at times filed in parallel sets of precinct trays in which the same precinct number will apply to both a larger and a smaller tray.

So much for current affidavits; now, to the canceled. The different western states have varying requirements as to how long county clerks must continue to store and keep available canceled voter registration forms. For searchers' purposes,

"There are remarkable physical re-
semblances, voice and mannerism similarities
among the women.

"And they are quick to point out mutual
interests that created moments when their lives
crossed or came close to it. Two of them had
used the same health spa as adults. Maureen
and Jan had both worked 'mucking out' stalls at
George Lee's Riding Stables for the privilege of
leading inexperienced riders on trail rides. Lucy
and Maureen just missed each other by two
weeks when they worked at a local auto
auction."

*—Report on three reunited sisters comparing
notes, as published in the June 19, 1978
South Bend, Indiana Tribune*

however, the time is in all cases too short. In California, for one,
it is no more than four years.

Fortunately, any county may hold the material for longer
periods if it so chooses. Many do. Each jurisdiction is then
entitled to establish its own procedures for affidavit retrieval. A
clerk in the affidavit office will be able to explain those steps
clearly.

In contrast to the free access to current voter registration
affidavits, nominal costs are normally involved in the retrieval
of canceled affidavits.

DEPARTMENT OF MOTOR VEHICLES

Among the eight western states in which the primary research for this manual was conducted, no one question re-

sulted in as much confusion within the civil bureaucracies as that regarding the public availability of information contained on driver's license and vehicle registration forms. Telephone calls were switched mercilessly from office to office to office. Forms and pamphlets mailed out in response to inquiries were, on delivery, revealed to have nothing to do with the requested material. It was that kind of project.

The proper regulatory procedures can't be all that difficult. Many corporations, with auto insurance companies leading the list, commonly enjoy systematic and swift entry to various state DMV files. Apparently, in some jurisdictions, a substantially different set of departmental rules is at work for companies than for private citizens.

Fortunately, because of its enormous population and relatively high per capita number of searchers, California is not one of those jurisdictions. Neither is Nevada, where the record services personnel are wonderfully pleasant and responsive.

The California Department of Motor Vehicles is among the many government bodies affected by the provisions and restrictions of the Golden State's 1968 Public Records Act. In accordance with the measure, the CDMV has made commendable efforts to establish simple, quick processes for individual access to data normally in its keeping. This material includes the residential address and other details customarily entered onto a driver's license and many of the details found in his or her driving record.

To make matters especially opportune for adult adoptees and birth parents, the departmental search for these documents can be conducted on the basis of a person's full name and birth date only, for a prepaid fee of 25 cents for the license and 75 cents for the driving record, and for a charge of 50 cents per page of photocopying. Ordinarily, no more than one page of photocopying is required in any single transaction.

Instructions for the proper use of the CDMV Information Request Service are provided by the Department in a free pamphlet efficiently titled "Department of Motor Vehicles Public Records Information." In its two pages, the pamphlet advises:

"Requests for records information from Vehicle and Vessel Records, Drivers License Records and Occupational License Records must be prepaid and submitted separately. Payment may be made by check, money order or information stamps. Requests must be made in writing on the proper form determined by the department. The department will refuse any request that is not submitted on the proper form . . ."

"Drivers License: (Requests must include either name and Drivers License number or full name and birth date and must be submitted on Form DL 15. Mail requests to P.O. Box 1231, Sacramento, CA 95806) . . . ."

"Stamps may be ordered in lots of ten stamps of 25¢ ($2.50), 50¢ ($5.00), 75¢ ($7.50), or $1.00 ($10.00) stamps . . . DL 15's are sold by the Department in lots of 100 for $1.47 per lot, tax included. Mail requests for information stamps and forms with check or money order to P.O. Box 1828, Sacramento, 95809. Enclose self-addressed envelope with requests for information stamps.

"Stamps may also be purchased from any local DMV field office."

As any of these procedures and costs may change slightly with time, it will always be safest to obtain a current copy of the instruction pamphlet from the California Department of Motor Vehicles Staff Services Section, 2415 First Avenue, Sacramento, California 95818.

In Nevada, DMV transactions are channeled through the Motor Vehicle Record Section, 555 Wright Way, Carson City, 89711. There, all requests for information must be made either in writing or in person. Nominal records search fees of two to five dolars are involved in the process, along with costs of one dollar per page for photocopying. If phoned in advance at (702) 885-5505, section personnel will mail out a fee schedule and some brief background material explaining their services.

SECTION III

With a name and an address in hand, events can move rather quickly. Already, several circumstances have been described that may bring searches very near to their conclusions: adoptive parents or delivery doctors may be personally acquainted with birth parents; a newspaper classified ad or mass mailing may reach the sought-after person; an appropriate current address might surface in a telephone directory, a city directory, a marriage certificate, probate records, or elsewhere. Soon, several more will be detailed.

When a search breaks, it invariably breaks suddenly. From one day to the next, adult adoptees patiently accumulate bits and pieces of search information while waiting for a decisive lead. Eventually it appears. One minute, they are still casting about for clues. Then, a letter is opened. A phone call is answered. The payoff arrives.

In response, searchers frequently find themselves momentarily lost in a pause. They may stare pensively at a telephone for several minutes, hesitating to make the final call. They may drive to a certain house, park, and sit wondering if it would be overly bold to walk to the front door, knock, and announce themselves. Many will spend some time alone attempting to get a grasp on what might happen next.

When the daze lifts, some will choose to avail themselves of the reunification intermediary services offered in a few states by civil agencies or by such private groups as the Washington Adoptees Rights Movement. But most will elect to take their own plunge into the unknown. At least, that's the pattern to date. For those who advance on the unknown, a reunification at its outset is something like a game played without any rules. They always reach a point after which advise and halfway measures give out and they're on their own.

Of course, a bit of politeness born of common sense will likely help. That's true everywhere and no less so here. When first contact is, say, by telephone, it will be advisable to begin by determining if the recipient of the call is positioned to talk freely. But beyond the obvious courtesies, there are no approaches that can be gradually taken to ease up on the initial moment of reunification. There are no tried and true opening lines capable of relieving the nervousness that characteristically attends the situation. The only real options lying in wait at the end of a search are to say "Hello," and reveal who you are, or to remain silent and anonymous.

Even at the last juncture, an exceedingly small fraction of the searcher population selects silence and anonymity. That's their decision to make. It's not up for critique. The choice does put certain apprehensions to rest.

In contrast, opt for "Hello" and what will then transpire is anybody's guess. Accumulate enough first-person stories, however, and a picture of the possibilities slowly emerges. The law of averages also begins to show its effect. Among searching adoptees, some will find parents of fame and position. Others will meet, finally, people broken by life's harsher afflictions. Immediately warm and rewarding reunifications await a few. Many will be kept at great emotional distances until the initial surprise wears off. Those are the extremes. But for the most part, it seems, reunions occur between adult adoptees and a middle range of shyly curious people who are reasonably cautious about the turn of events but who are willing to proceed onward in new relationships with their relinquished offspring.

What happens from there is solely the business of the seeker and the sought, although both will frequently share some of the resulting details with friends and other interested parties. Reports that trickle in from the search movement suggest that a post-reunification experience amounts to a very free, highly improvised exchange. People trade biographical reminiscences. They smile and cry. They gradually develop a feeling for one another. On that basis, they determine what future course to follow.

I have yet to hear of a completely unrewarding reunification or of a searcher who ever fully regretted embarkation. There are stories in circulation of bitter disappointments and tales of meetings that were flat and uninteresting. But in every instance, some minimal satisfaction has always been expressed in such encapsulations as, "Well, at least now I know."

So, for the moment, circumstances seem to favor searchers. After a decade's surge of reunifications into the thousands, the probabilities are clear. Almost every quest eventually reaches its goal. Almost every reunification starts out with a positive emotional resonance that the participants are capable of sustaining. Most importantly, it appears that all adult adoptees and birth parents are inherently endowed with the emotional resources needed to fulfill the entire drama; if there is a reason to think otherwise, it hasn't surfaced yet.

At this crossroad, more tips and techniques have been supplied to adult adoptees than will be required to complete most searches. For those that remain unfinished, however, the additional crop of research possibilities that follows may prove useful. It includes such alternatives as the Federal Social Security Administration, knocking on neighborhood doors, search self-help organizations, the assessor's office, the Veterans Administration, and tracing people through their jobs. To those:

SOCIAL SECURITY ADMINISTRATION

The Federal Social Security Administration is popularly known as the government body whose primary responsibility is to oversee the development of one form of retirement income for the major portion of America's working population. And that is all that most people know about the agency. So the overwhelming majority of searchers who I counsel are surprised when they hear the following:

Housed in the Social Security Administration is an

underpublicized, underappreciated department that is empowered to provide assistance, wherever possible, to individuals
seeking other individuals whose whereabouts within the
country are unknown. The respective parties may be old col-
lege friends who have lost touch with one another. Or similarly
situated army buddies. Or adoptees and their birth parents
and siblings. The official methodology for facilitating renewed
contact is indirect, time-consuming, and enormously effective.

It was through the good offices of this department that a
letter containing my name, address, and phone number, plus
a request to write or call, was forwarded to my half-brother. On
the basis of his immediate response, my search for him and
my birth mother was finally completed.

Given a relatively small collection of facts, any searcher may
avail himself or herself of this service. Significantly, though the
person being sought must have a social security number for
this opportunity to prove fruitful, that number is not a required
part of the necessary information that a searcher must forward
to the SSA.

In my instance, I presented the agency with nothing more
than my half-brother's name, the approximate year of his birth,
the approximate years in which he served in the military, and
our birth mother's name. But for other inquirers, other facts
will work equally well provided they are closely related to a birth
relative's chronological and economic history.

In deference to philosophically complicated questions surrounding notions of the right of privacy, the Social Security
Administration will never supply a searcher with the address of
the sought-after party. Instead, it implements this system
through a short series of letters that leaves the second party
with an unencumbered choice of whether or not to respond.

The entire process is initiated by a letter formally requesting
assistance mailed by a searcher to the federal agency. Ideally,
this correspondence should include as many hard facts as
possible describing the person with whom you are hoping to
connect; a brief, clear statement as to why you want to make
the connection, and an address or phone number suitable for
response.

"When her grandfather answered the door, Mrs. Dyer first introduced herself as 'Suzanne Dyer from Lake Jackson, Texas, and I'm trying to find some relatives.'

"Unbeknown to Mrs. Dyer, the grandfather had a reputation for his interest in genealogy. The elderly man thought Mrs. Dyer was visiting him for information on root-tracing.

"As they continued to chat, however, Mrs. Dyer confessed to him the true reason for her visit.

"'He tried to laugh about it at first, but I looked straight at him and said, "You are my grandfather, aren't you?" He said, "Yes, I am."'"

—From the April 23, 1978
Houston, Texas Chronicle

On receipt of the missive, SSA personnel will carefully attempt to identify this person in their very extensive, very well-organized files. Their success rate runs very high. When the identification is made, they will write two additional letters.

The first of these, in this case, will be to a searcher's birth relative. It will basically repeat much of the information pertaining to the desire for contact contained in the original correspondence to the Social Security Administration. But it will further stipulate that even though the message is being forwarded through the government, there is no legal obligation to reply.

The second will be to the searcher. It will inform him or her that identification has been made and that an agency correspondence has been mailed. It usually will also supply a short bit of advice along lines similar to what was presented to me: "We can give no assurance that our letter will be received or that you will get a response. In any case, we will not send (another) letter."

And so then begins the patient wait for response from the sought-after birth relative.

One caution in these proceedings. It seems that there are several desks within the Social Security Administration at which this kind of request is handled. Apparently not all the personnel at them are comfortable with the idea of contributing to a reunification effort. On very rare occasions, I have heard of a searcher's request returned without action on the grounds that it is "inappropriate," or for some such other excuse. The solution to this dilemma is simply to repeat the process anew on the very strong likelihood that another correspondence will find its way into more sympathetic hands.

Letters of inquiry to the Social Security Administration should be addressed to the attention of "Location Services" and posted to its national headquarters:

Social Security Administration
6401 Security Boulevard
Baltimore, Maryland 21235

Agency procedures governing this service may change slightly from time to time. As a result, before corresponding with Maryland, it is best to verify the steps to be taken with the nearest branch of the bureau's more than 1300 local offices or with one of its two west coast regional centers:

Region IX
(Arizona, California, Guam, Hawaii, Nevada)
Social Security Administration
100 Van Ness Avenue
San Francisco, California 94102
(415) 556-4910

Region X
(Alaska, Idaho, Oregon, Washington)
Social Security Administration
1321 2nd Avenue
Seattle, Washington 98101
(206) 399-0417

KNOCKING ON NEIGHBORHOOD DOORS

During the progress of my search, I successfully sought out a foster family with whom I had spent the six years of my life ranging from ages two through seven. The technique that I employed involved the modest expedient of returning to the neighborhood where we had all lived during those years to knock on a succession of doors in an effort to locate residents of long standing who might know something of my former parents' whereabouts.

What followed was absolutely marvelous. The next day I made telephone contact with my foster family and a week later we all gathered together once again for an afternoon's reunion. And in addition to the warmth and spirit that made the occasion worthwhile for its own sake, my foster parents recalled a few details about my past that were beneficial elsewhere in my search.

If the general talk emanating from the search movement can be trusted as a reliable measure, and I certainly have no cause to quarrel with it, this action of knocking on neighborhood doors appears to be an exceedingly efficient method of following the footsteps of birth relatives into the present. It also seems to account for a fair number of the surprises legendary among searchers and often mandates some very quick thinking as when—and this has happened—the person answering the door unexpectedly turns out to be an aunt or uncle by birth.

From my own brief experiences with this search technique, and from listening to tales of its application by others, it's evident that the strangers upon whose doors the knocks sound are ordinarily quite willing to respond to questions, provided that they are briefly advised of the purposes behind the inquiry and treated with appropriate politeness.

Following an opening introduction, the first courtesy to be extended should be a query as to whether or not the visit is convenient. If inconvenient, a return at another time should be suggested. Beyond that, a searcher has to play the situation as it happens.

SEARCH SELF-HELP ORGANIZATIONS

Search self-help and search support organizations are proliferating throughout the United States and Canada, and on the European and Asiatic sides of both oceans, faster than a full inventory of them can be maintained. Their services are recommended as frequently indispensable to the success of a search, but they come recommended with severe hesitations. Here's why on both counts:

Less than a decade ago, there existed in this country only two search organizations of note, Jean Paton's Colorado-based Orphan Voyage and Florence Fisher's New York-headquartered Adoptee's Liberty Movement Association, now The ALMA Society. Both enjoyed only limited influence outside their founding territories.

Currently, the last tally of search self-help groups that passed over my desk listed more than 90 regional, national, and international activist bodies, with the highly autonomous chapters of some of the more prominent organizations included in the inventory. Collectively, the mere fact of their numbers has given each an impact and added efficiency far beyond that which would have been achieved singularly.

The western states, naturally enough, have contributed their fair share to this ferment. In California particularly, the ALMA Society and other national search and support bodies have flourished. Throughout the western states, still other groups have emerged as a result of native impetus.

At their best, these organizations provide searchers with assistance that is invaluable. Through their auspices, adult adoptees and birth parents can often locate individuals in geographically distant areas who will help with research that would otherwise be impractical. Their search counselors can help interpret search data and outline futher research plans. Their members supply highly beneficial moral support to one another. Finally, a very few of these associations maintain search registries: complex, sophisticated mechanisms whereby adoptees and their birth parents may be reunited through the correlation of personal background information.

Given those benefits, what's the problem? Just this:

Many of the search groups all too readily repeat the mistakes common to activist organizations of all stripes. Some of them display a tendency to let organizational considerations become more important than the service to their members that justifies their existence. Movement leaders occasionally indulge in the very behavior they decry in those whom they consider to be the opposition; in this instance, they fall into the trap of acting exactly like the worst kind of social workers, attempting to answer for others such questions as if, when, and how a search should progress. They frequently divert enormous amounts of resources into interorganizational philosophical differences rather than channeling them into the more pressing tasks at hand.

Further, as an example of a difficulty peculiarly its own, the search and reunification movement suffers from unfortunate streaks of antiadoptive parent sentiment running through the ranks of its leadership, attitudes expressed not as espoused doctrine but rather as quick asides and glib slights. When properly viewed, ill will towards anyone is inherently at crosspurposes with what the adult adoptee-birth parent reunification movement is all about, which in its most basic guise is no more and no less than the fuller expression of love.

Nonetheless, for all these considerations, the search self-help groups do provide adult adoptees and birth parents with aid and services found nowhere else and the weaknesses to which these associations are vulnerable are not so pronounced as to outweigh their advantages. It is simply preferable that they be joined with one's eyes wide open, but then, that is also how a search should be conducted in its entirety.

Nominal fees, rarely amounting to more than $25 annually, are generally associated with membership in self-help groups.

At the local level, search organization leadership, mailing addresses, and telephone numbers typically change with such rapidity that no listing of them could hope to be accurate for more than four or five months. There are a few groups, however, large, stable and informed enough that they can refer an inquiring adult adoptee or birth parent to one of their affiliate chapters or to a regional search body of one sort of another.

The ALMA Society is a national organization with chapters in more than a dozen states. The Massachusetts-headquartered Concerned United Birthparents, the leading support group for men and women who have relinquished children for adoption, is similar in its scope. Nevada's International Soundex Reunion Registry and California's Triadoption Library regularly update their lists of the country's various search organizations. They will provide referrals whenever possible. The Washington Adoptive Rights Movement is a strong, statewide group.

Current addresses for these bodies are as follows:

The ALMA Society
  P.O. Box 154
  Washington Bridge Station
  New York, New York
  10033

Concerned United Birthparents
  P.O. Box 573
  Milford, Massachusetts
  01757

International Soundex Reunion Registry
  P.O. Box 2312
  Carson City, Nevada
  89701

"'Yes, yes,' I said. My mind was spinning. For a split second I thought it was a horrible joke someone was playing. The woman went on. 'I am sorry to tell you that your mother is dead but your grandmother is standing beside me and would like to talk to you.'

"My heart was pounding and tears were already streaming down my face. The next voice I heard was my grandma's. 'Hello my dear.' 'Grandma, is that really you?' 'Yes Valerie, it is. I have waited such a long time to talk to you.'"

—*Culmination of a search by telephone as reported in the July 20, 1978 Simi Valley, California Enterprise Sun & News*

Triadoption Library
P.O. Box 5218
Huntington Beach, California
92646

Washington Adoptees Rights Movement
305 South 43rd Street
GNC Room 20
Renton, Washington
98822

THE ASSESSOR'S OFFICE

To most adults, the county tax assessor's office is known only as the civic department from which property tax assessments emerge on an annual basis. To real estate agents, the office is additionally a bountiful and necessary professional resource. To adoptees in quest of their birth relatives, it can also supply valuable historical clues to the puzzles of the present.

In terms of contributing current information, however, there's very little that an assessor's office can do to advance a search. If you already have the names and present address of the relevant people in your past, there will be very little point in going to this office to look them up again. What it can supply are the names of people who may have known your birth relatives years ago. With luck, these people can help you steer you way from then forward.

Let's clarify this opportunity somewhat through the construction of a search scenario:

Assume that from an amended or original birth certificate you have identified the general area in which you were born. Assume further that from the certificate, a record of birth, or another source, that you have also discovered your initial surname. Any person in the ascertained locality bearing the same surname might be one of your birth relatives.

Given that possibility, your next step would be to scan all the city directories of that region—remembering that your birth parents may have resided in one town and had you delivered nearby in another—that correspond to your birth year and make a list, with addresses, of the similar surname people found therein. It would also be useful to follow the directories up the years and note when those people cease to be entries. The omission may indicate a move out of the area; a trip to the assessor's office then becomes potentially productive. Or the person may be deceased, which can be checked out with the state vital statistics office of the county probate department.

The information waiting at an assessor's office that is of interest to searchers is entirely public record. In operation, two systems of making this data openly available generally predominate. With the first, material is divided between display maps and a series of folios, all of which are housed on the public side of the clerk's counter and may be reviewed without procedural assistance. With the second, some material is imprinted in folios and onto microfilms, both of which require a clerk's assistance for location and viewing.

Regardless of the system, the first goal of a searcher at an assessor's office will be to take whatever addresses he or she has uncovered and correlate them with a block or tract number (as used here the terms are essentially equivalent) and a lot number, designations by which almost all privately owned parcels of land may be described. Under jurisdictions such as, say, San Francisco, the block number can be taken off a city map posted for this very purpose and a lot number can be found in a folio series known as the Secured Assessment Roll that is indexed by block numbers. In other areas, the details can be obtained from microfilm.

With the block and lot numbers determined, a searcher must then look to another folio series titled *Sales Ledger,* which is indexed by decades and block numbers. Through a careful review of these ledger's contents, it is possible to discover the names of every owner of the property at the time when the similar surname person being sought was residing there.

From out of these discoveries, additional well-defined avenues of research develop because the relationships that people can have with a residential address are very limited. Normally, they either owned or rented a home there.

If the former option was true and the potential birth relative being sought no longer resides at the given address, then most likely the house was sold. Reasonable chances exist that the new owner will remember something of the whereabouts of the previous one. Should the house have been sold repeatedly, then any one particular owner may have to be traced through the further use of city and telephone directories.

If the residence was rented, then landlords or apartment building managers should be approached for whatever help they might provide.

In all instances, however, a personal visit or correspondence with the homeowner or landlord will be the final step in this particular search process.

The address of the local assessor's office is regularly listed in the white pages of the telphone book under the general heading of county government offices. At present, no fees are connected with research there.

VETERANS ADMINISTRATION

The Federal Veterans Administration has been entrusted with the responsibility of overseeing and managing the many benefits that Congress has provided for the men and women who served in the country's national armed forces during the time of a declared or undeclared war.

To competently fulfill various statutory duties, the VA keeps reasonably concise records bearing in one way or another on the people with whom it is concerned. Some of the material is naturally of particular interest to searchers.

Interesting or not, the Veterans Administration is very tight-lipped regarding the information under its control. Repeated telephone calls to its offices have elicited a steady stream of denials that any facts and figures can be released without the consent of the involved veteran.

The denials are not quite correct. Some data is required by law to be given out on request. According to section 1.502 of the Veterans Administration's Freedom of Information Act compliance guidelines:

> "The monthly rate of pension, compensation, dependency and indemnity compensation, retirement pay, subsistence allowance, or educational allowance to any beneficiary shall be made known to any person who applies for such information."

By deduction, any positive response to a correspondence applying for those details will automatically reveal more than it says. It will affirm that the individual being sought is alive. It will verify that he or she did serve in the military. It will disclose, beyond the fact of military service, why he or she is eligible for VA attention: retirement, entrance into a formal academic program, and the like.

Those are all important considerations. They may lead to a letter-writing campaign to the people administering veterans admission programs at various colleges and universities. They

> "Mrs. Allen, after the nerves wore off a bit, says she was pleased her daughter had found her. Realizing her mother was nervous, Mrs. Poursartip knew she had to be reassuring.
>
> "'I told her I loved her, and told her never to feel guilty,' she says. 'I said "don't ever put yourself down."'"
>
> —*From the August 14, 1978*
> *Hayward, California* Daily Review

may prompt an appeal for additional information to civilian groups such as the Veterans of Foreign Wars. They would certainly be useful to include in letters to the Social Security Administration. As happens time and time again in searches, one fact can point the way to another.

Requests to the VA, which will probably have to refer to its Freedom of Information Act guidelines, may be made through its following national or regional offices:

National
Veterans Administration Central Office
810 Vermont Avenue
Washington, D.C., 20420

Alaska
Veterans Administration
P.O. Box 1288
Juneau, 99802

Arizona
Veterans Administration
3225 North Central Avenue
Phoenix, 85012

California
Veterans Administration
  11000 Wilshire Boulevard
  Los Angeles, 90024

Veterans Administration
  2022 Camino Del Rio North
  San Diego, 92108

Veterans Administration
  211 Main Street
  San Francisco, 94105

Hawaii
Veterans Administration
  P.O. Box 50188
  Honolulu, 96850

Idaho
Veterans Administration
  550 West Fort Street
  Box 044
  Boise, 83724

Nevada
Veterans Administration
  1201 Terminal Way
  Reno, 89520

Oregon
Veterans Adminstration
  1220 Southwest Third Avenue
  Portland, 97204

Washington
Veterans Administration
  915 2nd Avenue
  Seattle, 98174

JOB OPPORTUNITIES

Occasionally, the processes of research turn up the fact of a birth relative's professional capacity. In city directories, whenever the detail is available, it is listed with an entrant's name. It might be included in the background information contained in an adoption file. However and wherever the item arises, further means of advancing toward reunification frequently accompany its disclosure.

For example, a birth parent who once worked for the United States government may still be so employed. On the strength of that possibility, the United States Civil Service Commission becomes a potential source of additional search data. The Commission plays a major role in the qualifications testing, hiring, and professional advancement of most persons on the payroll of most U.S. government administrative departments. The military is the most prominent exception to its predominance.

Within the guidelines established in accordance with the national Freedom of Information Act, and with certain exceptions, the Commission is legally required to release on request a few specifics pertaining to individuals retained through its auspices. According to regulations, "The name, position title, grade, salary, and duty station of a Government employee is information available to the public . . . ."

That's not much. But if a birth parent is on federal government salary, the knowledge of his or her duty station immediately reveals the general area where he or she can be reached during business hours. To searching adoptees, that's everything.

The Commission is empowered to charge "a fair and equitable fee" for clerical time consumed in fulfilling an informational request. Business with it may be conducted by mail, through the following west coast addresses:

United States Civil Service Commission
  Federal Building   P.O. Box 36010
  450 Golden Gate Avenue
  San Francisco, California 94102

United States Civil Service Commission
302 Federal Office Building
First Avenue and Madison Street
Seattle, Washington 98104

A second example of how occupational details can assist a search is found in the general realm of professional directories. These are massive and thorough reference works that are regularly compiled and published by an extraordinarily large number of associations, boards, and institutes for the primary benefit of each body's affiliate members.

The primary content of these tomes is an extended listing of all persons sharing either a common employment or organization membership status. Each entry is normally accompanied by a cluster of information composed of brief bits of data that may include: the year of an entrant's birth, the year in which a professional academic degree was granted, the academic institution's name, the entrant's current business address and telephone number, his or her military rank and dates of service, if applicable, and the like.

Suppose, then, a birth parent is discovered to be a certified public accountant. The American Institute of Certified Public Accountants' *AICPA List of Members* contains the more than 120,000 names of its national and international membership along with each individual's business address.

Or, suppose a vocational designation is that of an electrical engineer. The *Institute of Electrical and Electronics Engineers Directory,* published by the world's largest engineering society, gathers together the names and business addresses of more than 170,000 affililates. In addition, for a society subcategory described as "Fellows," the directory material includes the entrants' dates and places of birth, the graduate degrees they have earned, the names of the academic institutions granting the degrees, and the years in which the degrees were granted.

Titles of potentially useful directories could run into the thousands, a condition verified by another thick reference vol-

> "'When it came to talking with her natural mother, she had reservations. 'I really expected her to say "go away." But when I introduced myself as her daughter she said, "I thought you would call. I knew that if you were anything like me you would contact me.'"
>
> —*From the April 20, 1978*
> *Arcata, California Union*

ume known as the *National Trade and Professional Associations of the United States and Canada and Labor Unions.* Now in its 15th year of publication by the Washington, D.C. company of Columbia Books, this weighty compilation currently lists more than 6000 organizations, any one of which may publish a directory of interest to a searching adoptee.

Frequently, the information found in professional directories is organized in accordance with a sequence of code numbers following immediately or shortly after a person's name. The codes generally operate in one of two ways. Either they supply immediate data, such as a birth year, or they provide a key to another section of the reference work. In both instances, a directory's introductory pages will always explain the meaning of various codes.

The *National Trade* giant is most often available in major metropolitan public libraries. Many professional directories can also be found there, as well as in occupational libraries maintained specifically for, say, law or medicine, or through a particular association's regional offices.

Finally, state governments irregularly publish vocational directories through whatever civil agency is responsible for testing, licensing, and maintaining standards of competence within a given profession. In California, for one, the agency is usually a subdivision of the Department of Consumer Affairs, a grouping of approximately 40 bodies that include the California State Board of Architectural Examiners, the State Board of Chiropractic Examiners, the Contractors' State License Board, the Psychology Examining Committee of the Board of Medical Quality Assurance, and so on.

There seems to be no fixed frequency requirements establishing when a state regulatory agency must publish a directory. Again in California, the only catalog of the Department of Consumer Affairs that is even approximately current is its 1979 *Directory of Professional Engineers and Land Surveyors.* Its last *Directory of Registered Nurses* was released in 1964.

Nonetheless, because both current and back issues of these volumes may provide such information as an entrant's home or business address at a given point in time, both can be useful to a search. They often sit on the shelves of state capital and major urban area public libraries.

EPILOGUE

"Go For It"

What's going on here? Over the past decade, an unforeseen restlessness has descended upon thousands of people who were once expected to regard certain aspects of their domestic lives with indifference. Today, they are mobile, active, inquiring, pursuing a goal that was once, for all practical purposes, forbidden. What is their larger purpose? What are their lasting effects?

Searchers are always advancing toward the heart of a mystery, whether they think in such terms or not. And probably most of them don't. I didn't until long after my reunification. But the mystery is continually there nonetheless. It's known as family.

Despite decades of academic and governmental effort, all modern attempts to distill the essence of what is meant by family into a few well packaged concepts (suitable for use by, say, social welfare bureaucracies) have failed. Philosophical inquiry has not conclusively established the full dimensions of family. Legislative hearings have not uncovered its many deeper meanings. In recent years, even the United States Supreme Court has chosen to differ severely with certain social welfare bureaucracies on the subject.

So intellectually and politically, the fundamental questions have endured without leading to answers that can be condensed into academic tracts or codified into statutes. And, of course, many of these most basic considerations are inseparable from whatever it is that is presently occurring with search and reunification. Can a child have two, or even three, sets of parents? What are the comparative values, if any, of genetic ties and emotional bonds? To what extent do blood lines bring people together into a common union? Is it all a matter of the spirit, or the flesh, or some combination of both?

It may often be expedient to take sides on these issues; it is not possible to resolve them conclusively in any widely applicable fashion. That conceptual elusiveness is one sign that a mystery, akin in its way to such transcendent concerns as love and faith, is at work here. But given that pursuit of a mystery is an essential part of search and reunification, then a possibility immediately surfaces to suggest that, as with matters of love and faith, perhaps it is really the responsibility of individuals to find their own answers to the questions posed by family.

For individuals, connection with a mystery classically occurs through means that are nonverbal and intuitive. Some would even go so far as to say that the process is spiritual. Such contact has a way of supplying "answers" to fundamental questions by virtue of making everything suddenly "feel" right. From that emotional state, a mystery can quickly transform into a bountiful source of inner satisfactions. But it can also be very demanding. It can insist that one make peace with it before peace can be found anywhere else.

Searchers are troubled by just such an insistence or they wouldn't be searching. They are prompted to settle something for themselves. That urging can hover around innocuously for years without attracting much attention. Then, without much forewarning, it becomes predominant. Its ascendancy is frequently triggered by a person's arrival at some pivotal juncture in his or her life: emergence into adulthood, marriage, divorce, the decision to have children. But no apparent reason for the change is necessary for the prompting to be decisive.

On the basis of the stirring, searchers set forth. Implicitly or explicitly, they are out to come to grips with some familial need that over the long run won't go away by itself. Obviously, the motivational specifics differ greatly from person to person. For searching adoptees, first causes are often encapsulated in the phrase, "the need to know." For searching birth parents, and

"In today's America, the 'nuclear family' is the pattern so often found in much of white suburbia. Sanden, Sociology: A Systematic Approach, p 320 (1965). The Constitution cannot be interpreted, however, to tolerate the imposition by government upon the rest of us of white suburbia's preference in patterns of family living .... The cited decisions recognized, as the court recognizes today, that the choice of the 'extended family' pattern is within the 'freedom of personal choice in matters of family life (that) is one of the liberties protected by the Due Process Clause of the Fourteenth Amendment.'"

—United States Supreme Court Justices Brennan and Marshall concurring in the 1977 Moore v. East Cleveland

birth mothers in particular, "the need to reconcile." But for both, short of outright suppression, the move toward reunification appears to be the only process capable of quieting the longings that arise out of the unknowns of biological connections.

In the process, they perform a valuable service for society. They bring a measure of the mystery of family into it. As probably no other secular group in the country is currently doing, searchers as a whole are making a living endorsement of the institution of the family by putting something of themselves on the line when they embark. They advance from a sense of conviction and commitment and concurrently reaffirm, for all who are interested, two essentials of domestic life.

For openers, they are saying that family counts. Initially, it may seem odd that so basic a principle would need much in the way of support. But many legislatures, and through them many social welfare bureaucracies, have seemingly forgotten its importance. Political figures as highly placed as Vice-President Walter Mondale and former HEW Secretary Joseph Califano have commented that sizeable portions of the greater body of American domestic relations law are antifamily and especially antifather. Their observations have sadly not had any appreciable effect on Congress or the states. Of all government bodies, only the United States Supreme Court has consistently shown enlightened respect for the sanctity of family.

Second, by their actions, searchers are declaring that they have a right to define their families as they choose. That principle is not so obvious. As a civil liberty, this prerogative has long been obscured by the contrivances of bureaucratic convenience and convention. But while government may be entitled to draw certain lines to insure the effective operation of, say, social assistance programs to the needy, that does not justify its further intrusion into areas where its intervention serves no purpose. And the imposition of sealed records laws on adults is but one sterling example of that kind of intrusion.

Choice in family matters means that adoptive parents and birth parents can share an overlapping relationship with an adoptee. It means that adoptees don't have to distinguish between their birth and adoptive siblings; they can all be one's brothers and sisters. In fact, the option to exercise this freedom may constitute the only opportunity by which the differing forms that family takes—family that originates from genetic succession, family that develops with personal upbringing, and family that emerges from the heart—can be integrated away from conflict and toward unity.

Every attempted reunification inherently makes those two statements. Society is hopefully better for the energy expended in their making. Individual searchers certainly benefit profoundly from the effort. Though their gains may not be externally dramatic or readily visible to any other person, very few adult adoptees and birth parents, apparently, complete their searches without subsequently reporting that the experience has contributed something deeply worthwhile to their lives. There are rewards awaiting those who follow mysteries to their conclusions. In the end, the results may not correspond to anything that was expected in the beginning, but they are invariably highly prized nonetheless.

The rewards entailed by a search and reunification most commonly have something to do with the cultivation and nourishment of self-confidence. Properly viewed, the detective work required of searching adult adoptees and birth parents represents an extended exercise in practical problem solving. As fact after fact is uncovered, the activity becomes increasingly reinforcing. Searchers teach themselves that they are capable of functioning well, in pursuit of their own goals, in a highly complex society.

But beyond the lessons of technique, an even deeper sense of self-confidence abides. As a search moves towards completion, previously enduring sensations of emotional restlessness commonly begin to fade. Certain puzzling attitudes bearing on personal identity begin to clarify. New images of one's place in the world slowly take form. Problems don't ncessarily disappear. New difficulties may crop up. There can be a great deal of exacting trial involved in working out a reunification. But one day, a change becomes inwardly tangible. You discover that you are to some degree a new person, in a slightly better, slightly more enjoyable fashion. You find that you are a person in whom you can have more faith. If searching is really about any one thing, it is about the ability to believe in yourself. Go for it.

APPENDIX

Major western states libraries containing reference works of interest to searchers.

ALASKA
Alaska State Library
State Office Building
Pouch G
Juneau, 99811

Z.J. Loussac Public Library
427 F Street
Anchorage, 99501

ARIZONA
Arizona State Library
1700 West Washington
State Capitol
Phoenix, 85007

Flagstaff City—Coconino County
Public Library System
11 West Cherry Street
Flagstaff, 86001

Phoenix Public Library
12 East McDowell Road
Phoenix, 85004

CALIFORNIA
California State Library
Library & Courts Building
Ninth & N Street
P.O. Box 2037
Sacramento, 95809

Los Angeles County
Public Library System
320 West Temple Street
P.O. Box 111
Los Angeles, 90053

Los Angeles Public Library
630 West Fifth Street
Los Angeles, 90071

San Diego County Library
5555 Overland Avenue
Building 15
San Diego, 92123

San Francisco Public Library
Civic Center
McAllister and Polk Streets
San Francisco, 94102

San Jose Public Library
180 West San Carlos Street
San Jose, 95113

Stockton-San Joaquin County
Public Library
605 North El Dorado Street
Stockton, 95202

HAWAII
Hawaii State Library
478 South King Street
Honolulu, 96813

IDAHO
Idaho State Library
325 West State Street
Boise, 83702

Boise Public Library
& Information Center
715 Capitol Boulevard
Boise, 83706

NEVADA
Nevada State Library
  401 North Carson Street
  Capitol Complex
  Carson City, 89710

Clark County Library
  1401 East Flamingo Road
  Las Vegas, 89109

Washoe County Library
  301 South Center Street
  P.O. Box 2151
  Reno, 89505

OREGON
Oregon State Library
  State Library Building
  Summer & Court Streets
  Salem, 97310

Library Association of Portland
  Multnomah County Library
  801 Southwest Tenth Avenue
  Portland, 97205

Salem Public Library
  585 Liberty Street Southeast
  Salem, 97301

WASHINGTON
Washington State Library
  Capital Campus (near 15th & Water)
  Olympia, 98504

King County Library System
  300 Eighth North
  Seattle, 98109

Date _____

The following material is requested on Interlibrary Loan

    AUTHOR _____

    TITLE _____

    PUBLISHER, PLACE OR PUBLICATION AND DATE (Or title of periodical, volume and year)

    _____

    VERIFIED IN: _____

    TO BE BORROWED FROM: _____

I agree to pay all postage and insurance charges connected with the above loan and take full responsibility for care and prompt return of the book.

    PRINT NAME _____

    ADDRESS _____

    TELEPHONE _____   DATE CARD EXPIRES _____

    INIT.: _____   SIGNATURE _____

                Not needed after:

For I.L.L. Librarian's use only:

                        Borrowed from:

- CC Auth
- CC Title
- NUC PRE-56
- Holding
- NUC
- UCLA DICT CAT 1919-62
- UC DICT DAT 1963-67
- UCB DICT CAT
- CBI
- BIP
- ULS
- NST
- Newspapers in microform

    OTHER:

Sample interlibrary loan form as mentioned under Section I subheading, "Newspaper Vital Statistics Announcements."

SUPERIOR COURT OF CALIFORNIA, COUNTY OF SAN FRANCISCO

In the Matter of (minor's name)

Case Number

APPLICATION AND ORDER FOR APPROVAL OF THE COURT T
OBTAIN INFORMATION REGARDING AN ADOPTION

For the reasons set forth below, permission is hereby sought   (check pertinent statement)

_____ to determine whether an action has been filed for the adoption of the party whose name is shown above:

_____ to obtain a certified copy of decree.   (check the pertinent statement;)

_____ other:

Other name by which child known: _____

Name of adopting parents: _____

Date of adoption _____   *(C.C. 227 prohibits release of any adoption information "except in exceptional circumstances and for good cause approaching the necessitous.")*

Reason for request: _____

_____

_____

(Use other side if more room needed)

I am _____
       (Here give information identifying applicant and relationship to above parties)

Name: Address:
Dated: City & State:

                                   Telephone No.
                                   Dated:
_____   At   , California
          (Signature)
Subscribed and sworn to before me   I certify (or declare) under penalty of perjury that the
                                    foregoing is true and correct.
day of   , 19

(SEAL)   Notary Public   _____
                                            (Signature)

NOTE: The form of declaration under penalty of perjury to be used only when executed in the State of California. If document is
       executed outside the State of California, the affidavit form is to be executed before a notary public or other officer authorized
       to administer oaths.

ORDER
Good cause appearing therefor, permission is hereby granted the above named applicant to obtain the information and
the services hereinabove set forth. The Court finds that the requirements of Civil Code Section 227 have been met.

Dated _____ , 19_____

                                   _____
                                            Judge

APPLICATION AND ORDER FOR APPROVAL OF THE COURT TO OBTAIN
INFORMATION REGARDING AN ADOPTION

76A6200 - (Rev. 1-74) 1-74

Sample court petition as mentioned under Section I
subheading "Sealed Records Files."

95

The following is reprinted in its entirety from the January 22, 1978 California Living magazine of the Sunday Examiner & Chronicle:

Piecing The Past Together

by Hal Aigner

"Dear Hal,

"Sorry for the delay in answering your letter, but I guess the answer is negative. I'm fifty-two, so I can't be your brother, and my family all come from Florida and Rhode Island. The other names you mention are not known to me either.

"Sorry I can't be of more help, and good luck in your quest."

"Dear Hal,

"Received your letter last week. I don't believe we can help you at all as none of those names register the tiniest bit of light. I can give you a rundown on our family history (three pages) . . . Just this past year I also received a letter from an elderly woman who turned out to be the youngest daughter of the people who adopted dad. (She was born after dad left his adoptive parents.) So there's hope."

For ten months, letters like these trickled in to me at a slight but steady rate. Inevitably the information they contained was scant. But I was locked into a search for a full eight years of my life and as sources of encouragement, these messages proved invaluable.

They were responses to inquiries I had mailed out by the hundreds. At thirty-two, as an adoptee who had not seen his biological mother for twenty-three years or his biological father ever, I had decided to embark on a search for my origins. There are an estimated five million adoptees in this country, about half of whom are placed in what is termed a "nonrelative" adoption, and thousands are currently engaged in similar pursuit. We all quickly learn that massive postal campaigns are simply part of good search technique.

Some personal details are required here. I was born out of wedlock at a time when cruel liabilities accompanied single parenthood. I was soon placed in what became a series of foster homes. By age eight, I was with my fourth family. I visited my biological mother irregularly until age nine. At eleven, I was finally adopted.

Slightly more than two decades later, several beneficial years in psychiatry brought me face to face with my need to search for my past. The motivations that surfaced so clearly do not easily reduce to abstractions. I wanted answers. I wanted facts. Like the proverbial itch that needs scratching, a curiosity fueled by an almost existential sense of incompleteness, and a strange growing anger that was new to me, demanded action. To the person standing in my shoes, there was really no other way to go.

So letters became important. Compared to other adoptees I was soon to meet, I started with a wealth of details. Though the passing years had blurred many facts in my memory, I quickly assembled the names of my biological parents and a half brother whom I had once met, the approximate dates of several personally significant life events, and some geographical specifics. Names, above all else, pre-ordain certain kinds of extraordinarily tedious work. Here's how part of that goes:

In most metropolitan areas, at least one branch of the Bell System provides public access to every telephone book in the country. Searchers will spend days in these directories, addressing envelopes to every person coast to coast with surnames matching those of sought after individuals. They insert into each a photocopied form letter, lick and apply yet another stamp, and add it to the heap destined for the evening mail. All the while, they thank some lucky star they were not born a Smith or a Jones. (Perfectly nice names, but still.) If this labor in any way resembles true detective work, then the sleuthing profession must be burdened by some ungodly stretches of boredom.

As searchers wait for replies, they're not idle. They join search self-help organizations such as ALMA, the Adoptees' Liberty Movement Association, listed in the San Francisco phone book. They take the names to historical societies, trade unions, church registries. Sure, they know that in any one encounter, the odds are running high against them. But eventually, something has to turn up.

The first big payoff that came to me, though . . . well, it arrived in the mail and it was one of the chances you take by beginning this process.

"Dear Mr. Aigner,

"We think the man who was likely your father died three years ago in Winnemucca, Nevada. At the time, he was about seventy years old and was a carpenter. He had been a sailor and had lived in Reno. He came from Ainhice-Mongoles in France's Basque country . . ."

The facts checked out. These few final words did not describe the best of what I had hoped to find. They provided answers nonetheless. But with this correspondence, a chill descended on me. Maybe I was going to arrive too late all the way around.

Fortunately, my adoptive parents were now backing my efforts, primarily with timely and welcome moral support. This occurs in searches rather frequently. While adoptive parents rarely appear fully at east with reunifications—in fact, some have organized pressure groups and bitterly oppose the practice—many join in quite readily. A San Francisco friends' eighty-six year old adoptive father initially suggested her search. It's a part of the life experience he wants to share with her. These are true gifts.

The idea that adoptive parents in general are irremediably antagonistic to reunifications was only the first of several prominent adoption myths that evaporated as I advanced. In my progress, I eventually yielded to an increasing pressure I felt to explore this entire process that had so influenced my life.

From this point on, a formal study of adoption's history and procedures accompanied my search. What I discovered was profoundly disturbing.

What I found out let me to believe that adoption in America has been dehumanized to the point of scandal. True, as a purely statutory creation, it is only a subsection of a greater body of family law, but it is the part with which I was concerned.

From what I learned it seems to me that prospective adoptive parents suffer enormously at the hands of child placement agencies. Their efforts to extend their love to a child are often met with ignominious inquiries into physical sterility or infertility. Their dignity is invaded. Their privacy abused. To this day, these potential parents receive only occasionally adequate protection against the possibility of an agency removing a child from their home without notice or explanation before an adoption is finalized. California, happily, provides some exceptions to this rule.

The biological parents relinquishing a child fare equally badly, particularly the unmarried. Through very subtle measures such as punitive structuring of social services, selective investiture of parental rights, and arbitrary use of misdemeanor statures and sentencing, the law has almost guaranteed that many domestic difficulties will escalate into problems so severe that releasing a child for adoption is not so much a choice as an inevitability. In some localities, this traditional pattern meets with fierce resistance from unwed parents, but its power is still strong.

Adoptees, too, are burdened by the law and the placement agencies. Those of us who need to face the facts of our personal histories are deterred by the sealed records legislation enacted by every state except Alabama and Kansas. To the placement agency mentality, adoptees from eighteen to eighty are still "children" incapable of maturely living with these details. Our inquiries are shunted aside, and we're frequently told that our need to know is a sign of emotional disturbance.

Sealed records, however, are not the final words on the subject to reunifications. They weren't for me. Through a very

99

circuitous route, a letter reached my half brother. He phoned me immediately. And in those final few seconds, I discovered that my mother was living in a San Francisco retirement home, not six blocks from an apartment where I lived for a year.

What is that initial moment of reunification like? It's much like finding yourself in uncharted psychic territory. There are no rules. No norms govern the situation. There are no games to play, no mannered conversations to fall back on. And there's no middle ground, no halfway measure one can use to present gradually to an elderly woman the fact that this stranger contacting her is the son she hasn't seen for twenty-three years.

Luckily, I had the advantage of a dress rehearsal. In my search I had located a foster family with whom I had lived from ages two to six. When I got their phone number, I simply called, announced myself, and relaxed in the warmth of their excitement. We made plans for dinner. I arrived at their home and discovered they had anticipated the day I would return. They had saved a sizeable collection of my childhood mementos. Snapshots. First report cards. Even home movies. It was a joy.

Now, I repeated the process and with some trembling said, "Mother, this is Eddie" (the name she knew me by). Within two hours, we were together in the lobby of her retirement home. We hugged, talked, asked questions of each other. She spoke of her life, which was never easy, and of how my biological father was such a handsome man. She kept repeating, "I always knew one day you would come looking for me. I knew that any son of mine would one day come looking for me."

Her response as a mother accounted for one last major adoption myth vanishing before my experience. Opponents of reunifications are forever harping on the need to protect the privacy of the biological mother. Yet, there is a rapidly mounting body of evidence establishing that this need for protection is more imagined than real.

From numerous reports emerging out of the reunification movement, the overwhelming majority of contacted mothers—and here I'm talking upwards of 90 per cent—ultimately react with relief and enthusiasm. It's as if they can finally be free of something that has been gnawing at them for years.

This whole protection myth, I believe, is part of the repugnant sexual politics that creates victim roles for women. One never hears, for example, of the need to protect the privacy of the biological father.

If I was secretly harboring any pretenses of taking my reunification casually in stride, they were overwhelmed by the magnitude of the event. The impact of the moment went far beyond anything I had fantasized during my ten months of searching. I would like to share, as far as words can convey, a few of the effects.

My most surprising and immediate reaction was intensely physical. I literally emoted a strange warmth so forcefully that for several nights following I couldn't sleep under blankets, despite living in San Francisco's chilly Sunset District. Oddly, this radiance in no way resembled the mechanical body heat that hard work generates. It was more like a phosphorescence. More like a glow from a fire. I'm sure that to the right set of eyes I would have lit up the night.

For several days, I spent my waking hours enveloped in a sensation of being totally in the "here and now." While I'm generally wary of cosmic consciousness jargon, no other description fits this feeling. This experience of living comfortably in a present bereft of a relevant past or future was rare to me. I can't remember anything else ever resembling it.

Many changes were definable only in terms of what stopped happening. I had spent my years with an irritating tug from the past always disturbing my peace of mind. Soon after the reunification, I awoke one morning and realized this nuisance was gone. In its place was a lightness, an open airiness like something that often accompanies the disappearance of a severe migraine.

Finally, I savored—and this is a continuing delight—an enormous sense of victory over the forces that had meddled in my life for the eleven years it took me to reach the safety of my adoptive parents. To the viewpoint of a child unable to fathom the reasons why he was shifted among families, it seemed as if those forces were omnipotent. They had taken me from people I loved, from people who loved me to another home where I was loved equally well and richly, true, but the move itself was debilitating.

In the end, however, I was the one who healed the wounds and triumphed. The reunification, to be sure, was not the universal aspirin capable of relieving all the world's headaches. And, there is still much about my adoptive history that I have to work out within myself. But I had proved stronger than the passing years, growing distances, and impersonal bureaucracies.

My conscience, though, compels me to admit that there's a catch to this self-acclaimed story of great trials, brave deeds, and final glory: The opposition is usually a pushover.

Inhumane adoption procedures proliferate because the adoption triangle—the set of relationships defined by adoptees, their biological parents and their adoptive parents—acquiesces to their authority; almost always unnecessarily. When the members of the triangle recognize their own positions and creative possibilities, confusion clears, alternatives appear, and personal power takes form. Listen to another condensed but illustrative story:

Terry J., a San Franciscan of my acquaintance began a search for her biological mother in 1976.

"Minnesota, where I was placed in an orphanage, allows for some intermediation through a state agency. I stayed on the telephone for forty-five minutes with a caseworker back there and played good cop-bad cop with him. I'd be very demanding and insistent one minute and very sympathetic and supportive the next. I got a promise from him that he would let me know something by Christmas Eve. On that day I got a letter from Minnesota containing my mother's name and address in Seattle. I phoned her that night; I hadn't talked with her in all my forty-two years. It turned out she had started looking for me, too. Her greatest fear was that I would hate her for giving me up. I don't hate her at all; there's no animosity or barriers between us. We can be off to a clean start."

As my story circulates among my friends and their friends, questions on some aspect of adoption frequently filter back to me. My answers generally look like this:

In adoption, there is nothing inherently threatening to anyone except for the fear created by the social welfare bureaucracies. There are no problems so complex that their solution requires the massive governmental interference that the placement agencies represent. This is not a zero-sum game in which one party's gain is based on another's loss. I believe the entire system needs reordering in favor of the resources of the biological and adoptive parents. Then everyone will stand the best chances of winning.

In my opinion, the procedure is at a crossroads, because the bureaucracies are losing control. Prospective adoptive parents are demanding and receiving due process of law in the courts. Adoptees and biological parents in search are circumventing, quite lawfully, the sealed records laws that inhibit them from exploring their common pasts. Unwed parents no longer relinquish their children at the 90 per cent rate of recent years; that figure has dropped in some areas to about 10 per cent. And in this restoration of power to the adoption triangle, there is hope.

Biological parents and prospective adoptive parents can join together and plan a future for the child they both love. This happens. I have on file photocopies of recent court cases in which the former have appeared in support of the latter's petition. My feeling is that there would currently be far more adoptions if biological parents weren't hampered by a system insisting that they release their offspring into a great unknown.

Children have a right to reach majority in the most stable possible home environment. To biological parents of youngsters under eighteen, the search self-help organizations will extend personal counseling services but they will not help with detective work. They accurately contend that biological parents have no business contacting adoptees still in their youth.

But when adoptees reach majority, they are adults, a

distinction lost to regulatory thinking. If they desire the facts of their pasts, they have a right to full information as surely as they have a right to vote, marry, or seek employment of their choice. If the knowledge is possibly painful, well, a favored candidate may lose an election, a marriage may fail, a business may fold.

And perhaps most importantly, everyone in the adoption triangle simply needs to start feeling better. I am saddened by the number of adoptive parents I meet who have lost touch with the pride they are entitled to feel in their expanded role as parents and problem solvers. That adoption works at all, and by and large it works very well, is not because of bureaucractic procedures. It is successful because these mothers and fathers are, in the first and final analysis, mothers and fathers.

Similarly, adoptees who feel the need to search should proceed without the pangs of emotional doubts. If that's where you must go, it's a fine route to take. And biological parents should not worry about being found. No matter how deeply it may be buried, a searcher's foremost motivation is love.

And that, ultimately, is what adoption and its peripheral controversies are all about. The adoption triangle is bound together by this feeling. There's too much fear afoot in the world. But it's never so strong or frightening or dangerous, that love, even just a little love, can't get the best of it.